CONTRIBUTIONS TO ORIENTAL HISTORY AND PHILOLOGY
No. I

SUMERIAN HYMNS

FROM

CUNEIFORM TEXTS IN THE BRITISH MUSEUM

TRANSLITERATION, TRANSLATION
AND COMMENTARY

BY

FREDERICK AUGUSTUS VANDERBURGH, Ph.D.

New York
THE COLUMBIA UNIVERSITY PRESS
1908

PRINTED BY G. KREYSING, LEIPZIG, GERMANY

Note

The so-called "Sumerian Question" as to the genuine linguistic character of the ancient Non-Semitic Babylonian texts has agitated the Assyriological world for more than twenty years. The new Sumerian matter from the monuments which is constantly coming to hand demands, in the interest of all those who can look upon this discussion with impartial eyes, a most rigid and unprejudiced examination. Dr. Vanderburgh in the following monograph has adhered to the views expounded in my "Materials for a Sumerian Lexicon" (J. C. Hinrichs'sche Buchhandlung, 1905—1907), that the so-called Sumerian was originally a Non-Semitic agglutinative language which, in the course of many centuries of Semitic influences, became so incrusted with Semiticisms, most of them the result of a very gradual development of the earlier foreign sacred speech of the priests, that it is really not surprising to find the theory that Sumerian was merely a Semitic cryptography set forth and vigorously upheld by so eminent a scholar as Professor Halévy (MSL., pp. VIII, IX).

The study of the more ancient Non-Semitic texts, more particularly of the Sumerian unilingual hymns, cannot fail to shed additional light on the nature of this peculiar idiom, besides furnishing a valuable addition to the study of the Babylonian religious system.

The texts of the hymns in Vol. XV. of the Brit. Mus. Cun. Texts are not always in good condition and present many difficulties, a solution of some of which, it is hoped, has been suggested in this work with at least approximate correctness.

John Dyneley Prince

Columbia University
October 1st, 1907

To the

Rev. Edward Judson, D. D.,

in recognition of his friendship to the author
and of his interest in Oriental studies

Preface

Vol. XV. of the "Cuneiform Texts from Babylonian Tablets in the British Museum, printed by order of the Trustees", was published in 1902. Plates 7—30 of this valuable volume contain hymns addressed to Bêl, Nergal, Adad, Sin, Tammuz, Bau and Ningirgilu. Of these, besides the translations given in the present work, the following have been translated and commented on; viz, J. Dyneley Prince, Jour. Amer. Or. Soc., xxviii, pp. 168—182, a hymn to Nergal (Pl. 14); and a hymn to Sin (also rendered and explained in this thesis) by E. Guthrie Perry, in *Hymnen und Gebete an Sin* (Pl. 17). In press at present are also translations by J. D. Prince, a hymn to Bau, Vol. XV. Pl. 22 in the Harper Memorial Volume (Chicago); and, by the same author, a hymn to Ningirgilu, Vol. XV. Pl. 23, in the Paul Haupt Collection to appear in 1908.

All these hymns in Plates 7—30 stand by themselves as distinct from anything hitherto published. They are unilingual, a fact indicating that they are very ancient and furthermore adding materially to the difficulty of their translation. This Thesis ventures a transliteration, translation and commentary of four of the hymns which are peculiarly difficult owing to their unilingual Non-Semitic character. Of the history of the tablets in question, which are all in the Old Babylonian character, we have no information. They must tell their own story.

The writer of this Thesis wishes to acknowledge with much appreciation the aid given him by Dr. John Dyneley Prince, Professor of Semitic Languages in Columbia University, in the preparation of this work.

New York, Oct. 1st, 1907

F. A. Vanderburgh

List of Abbreviations

AL: Assyrische Lesestücke, von Friedrich Delitzsch. Vierte durchaus neu bearbeitete Auflage.
ASK: Akkadische und Sumerische Keilschrifttexte, von Paul Haupt
BN: Das Babylonische Nimrodepos, von Paul Haupt.
Br: A Classified List of Cuneiform Ideograms, Compiled by Rudolph E. Brunnow.
CDAL.: A Concise Dictionary of the Assyrian Language, by William Muss-Arnolt.
CḪ: The Code of Ḫammurabi, King of Babylon, by Robert Francis Harper.
Cler: Collection de Clercq Catalogue Antiquités Assyriennes.
CT: Cuneiform Texts from Babylonian Tablets in the British Museum.
Déc: Découvertes en Chaldée, par Ernest de Sarzec.
EBH: Early Babylonian History, by Hugo Radau.
EBL· Explorations in Bible Lands during the 19th Century, by H. V. Hilprecht.
HBA: A History of Babylonia and Assyria, by R. W. Rogers.
HW: Assyrisches Handwörterbuch, von Friedrich Delitzsch.
IG: The Great Cylinder Inscriptions A and B of Gudea, by Ira Maurice Price.
JA: Journal Asiatique.
JRAS: The Journal of the Royal Asiatic Society.
MSL: Materials for a Sumerian Lexicon, by John Dyneley Prince.
N: Nippur, or Explorations and Adventures on the Euphrates, by John Punnett Peters.
OBI: Old Babylonian Inscriptions, chiefly from Nippur. By H. V. Hilprecht
OBTR: Old Babylonian Temple Records, by Robert Julius Lau.
R: Cuneiform Inscriptions of Western Asia, prepared by Sir Henry Rawlinson.
RAAO: Revue d'Assyriologie et d'Archéologie Orientale.
RBA: Die Religion Babyloniens und Assyriens, von Morris Jastrow, Jr.

RSA: Recueil de Signes Archaiques de l'Écriture Cunéiforme, par V. Scheil.

SSD: Les Signes Sumériens derivés, par Paul Toscanne.

SSO: A Sketch of Semitic Origins, by George Aaron Barton

SVA: Die Sumerischen Verbal-Afformative nach den ältesten Keilinschriften, von Vincent Brummer

TC: Tableau Comparé des Écritures Babylonienne et Assyrienne Archaiques et Modernes, par A. Amiaud et L. Mechineau.

TEA: Der Tontafelfund von El Amarna, herausgegeben von Hugo Winckler.

TR: Travels and Researches in Chaldaea and Susiana, by Wm. K. Loftus.

Table of Contents

Introduction

The gods honored in the hymns treated in the following Thesis are Bêl, Sin (Nannar), Adad (Ramman) and Tammuz, all deities of the old Babylonian pantheon, representing different phases of personality and force, conceived of as incorporated in nature and as affecting the destinies of men. These gods are severally designated in the hymns as follows:

in Tablet 13963, Rev. 1, "O Bêl of the mountains;"
in Tablet 13930, Obv. 2, "O father Nannar;"
in Tablet 29631, Obv. 10, "O Ramman, king of heaven"; and
in Tablet 29628, Obv. 3, "The lord Tammuz" (CT. XV, 10, 15, 16, 17 and 19).

The attributes and deeds belonging to these divinities are adduced from a wide range of literature, beginning with the royal inscriptions of the pre-dynastic periods and ending with the inscriptions of the monarchs of the later Babylonian empire. In fact, the building inscriptions of the Babylonians, the war inscriptions of the Assyrians, the legendary literature, the incantations, as well as the religious collections, particularly the hymns, afford us many descriptions, of greater or less length, of all the Babylonian gods.

To aid the student in understanding better the character of the four gods whose hymns have been translated in the following Thesis, I here give a brief descriptive sketch of each of the deities whose praises were sung in the documents which I have chosen to render.

1. *Bêl*

Bêl was the most ancient of all Babylonian gods and was a popular deity through the historic rise and fall of several Babylonian states, when no other god received prominent recognition. When En-šag-kušanna, lord of Kêngi, subdued the city of Kiš in the north of Babylonia, he brought the spoil of his victory to Bêl. "To Bêl (*En-lil*), king of the lands, En-šag-kušanna, lord of Kêngi, the spoil

of Kîš, wicked of heart, he presented."[1] Urukagina, king of Lagaš, built a temple to Ningirsu, the god of Girsu, but he, in honoring Ningirsu as the hero of Bêl, was really honoring Bêl. "For Ningirsu, the hero of Bêl, Urukagina, king of Širpurla, his house he built."[2] Eannatum, who was patesi of Lagaš and made himself king of Kîš, calls himself the chosen of Bêl, as follows: "Eannatum, patesi of Širpurla, chosen of Bêl."[3] Entemena, who is called in the Vase of Silver, "son of Enanatum",[4] and who probably was the nephew of Eannatum, introduces his fine Cone Inscription with these words. "Bêl, king of the lands, father of the gods."[5] He also claims in the same inscription to derive the right to reign from Bêl: "Entemena, patesi of Širpurla, to whom a sceptre is given by Bêl."[6] Entemena's Cone also gives us information about Mesilim. It speaks of Mesilim as "king of Kîš."[7] In describing the victory of Mesilim over the Gišbanites, a people located apparently not very far from Kîš, Entemena tells us that the victory was effected by the command of Bêl. "Upon the command of Bêl a scourge he (Mesilim) brought over them (the Gišbanites); the dead in a field of the land he buried."[8] For map showing supposed location of Gišban, see SSO. p. 158. Lugalzaggisi, a usurper from the north, making himself master of the world in all directions and setting up a throne at Erech, in his inscription of 132 lines, freely recognizes the favor of Bêl. "Bêl, king of the lands, to Lugalzaggisi, king of Erech, the kingship of the world did give."[9] In this period preceding Sargon I., Šamaš seems to have a distinct place in the religious world, but he does not receive the attention that Bêl receives. He is particularly mentioned in one inscription; viz., in the *Stèle des Vautours,* where he is spoken of as "Šamaš, the king who dispenses splendour."[10]

---

[1] *dingir En-lil lugal kur-kur-ra En-šag-kuš-an-na en Ki-en-gi nig*(NI)-*ga Kiš-ki ḫul-šag a-mu-na-šub* (OBI. Nos. 90 and 92).

[2] *dingir Nin-gir-su gud dingir En-lil-lá-ra Uru-ka-gi-na lugal Šir-la-pur-ki-ge è-ni mu-na-ru* (Clercq II, Pl. viii, Col. I).

[3] *E-an-na-tum pa-te-si Šir-la-ki-pur-ge mu-pad-da dingir En-lil-ge* (Galet A, Col. I. See Déc. XLIII).

[4] *En-teme-na dumu En-an-na-tum* (Lines 3 and 10. See Déc. XLVII).

[5] *dingir En-lil lugal kur-kur-ra ab-ba dingir-dingir-ru-ne-ge* (Cone of Entemena, Col. I, 1—3. See Déc. XLVII).

[6] *En-teme-na pa-te-si Šir-la-pur-ki pa sum-ma dingir En-lil-lá* (Cone of Entemena, Col. V, 19—23. See Déc. XLVII).

[7] *Me-silim lugal Kiš-ki-ge* (Cone of Entemena, Col. I, 8—9. See Déc XLVII).

[8] *ka dingir En-lil-lá-ta sa-u-gal ne-u má*(SAR)-*dul-tak-bi edin-na ki-ba ni-uš-uš* (Cone of Entemena, Col. I, 28—31. See RAAO. Vol. IV, Plate II).

[9] *dingir En-lil lugal kur-kur-ra Lugal-zag-gi-si lugal Unug-ki-ga nam-lugal kalam-ma e-na-sum-ma-a* (OBI. No. 87, Col. I, 1—4 and 39—41).

[10] *dingir Babbar lugal zal sig-ga-ka* (see Déc. XXXVIII, Fragment D^1, middle of the Fragment).

The date of these early Babylonian rulers, of course, is, as yet, not accurately determined. The relative age of each is made out chiefly from palaeographic evidences (see EBH. p 8, for example), supplemented with the attempt at fitting into one harmonious whole the events which the inscriptions of these rulers divulge Then the whole schedule is crowded backward or forward or internally changed from time to time as new evidence is gathered for or against the testimony of Nabonidus (555—538 B. C) who, when he discovered the tablet of Narâm-Sin, declared that he was gazing on that which no eyes had beheld for thirty-two hundred years. Nabonidus says. "I dug to a depth of eighteen cubits, and the foundation of Narâm-Sin, the son of Sargon, which for thirty-two hundred years no king that had preceded me had discovered, Šamaš, the great Lord of E-barra, permitted me, even me, to behold."[1] On the supposed relation of these kings to Narâm-Sin, the rulers En-šag-kušanna, a king of the south, Urukagina, of Lagaš, and Mesilim, a king ruling at Kiš, are placed along about the date of 4500 B. C., while Eannatum, Enannatum and Entemena, successive rulers at Lagaš, are placed near the date of 4200 B C. Lugalzaggisi of Erech is placed at 4000 B. C. It may be stated here that the date of Sargon I. as 3800 B. C. is obtained by adding to 3200 the date of the reign of Nabonidus as 550 years B. C. and also the length of the reign of Sargon I. as 50 years.

The seat of Bêl's cult was Nippur, a city lying between the Euphrates and Tigris, a little below Babylon, and located, as it were, in the midway favorable to receiving homage from kings of either the north or the south of Babylonia. We find it mentioned as early as the time of Entemena, who in one of his inscriptions, in speaking of something presented to Bêl, says: "To Bêl of Nippur by Entemena it was presented".[2] In the bilingual legend of the Creation, Nippur seems to be regarded as a very old city. It is placed at the head of the list of three that are mentioned as ancient cities of Babylonia. "Nippur was not made; E-kur was not built. Erech was not made; E-anna was not built. The abyss was not made; Eridu was not built."[3] Nippur evidently is older than the worship of Bêl and the conception of Bêl is older than the first king of whom we have mention; viz., En-šag-kušanna, who is placed at 4500 B. C.

[1] (56 b) XVIII *amat ga-ga-ri* (57) *ú-šap-pi-il-ma te-me-en-na Na-râm-*[ilu] *Sin*(EŠ) *mâr Šar-ukin* (58) *šá* III M II C *šânâte ma-na-ma šarru a-lik maḫ-ri-ia la i-mu-ru* (59) [ilu] *Šamaš belu rabu-ú È-bar-ra* (60) *ú-kal-lim-an-ni ia-a-ši* (V R. 64, Col. II).

[2] *dingir En-lil-li En-lil-ki-ta En-te-me-na-ra mu-na-šub* (OBI. No. 116).

[3] *En-lil-*[ki] *nu-du È-kur-ra nu-dim Unug-*[ki] *nu-du È-an-na nu-dim zu-ab nu-du Nun-*[ki] *nu-dim* (CT. XIII, Tablet 82—5—22, 1048. Plate 35, lines 6, 7 and 8).

At Nippur was located Bêl's great temple which was commonly called E-kur, house of the mountain, a name particularly descriptive of the shrine of Bêl resting on the top of the mountain-like *ziggurrat.* Sargon I. calls himself the builder of Bêl's temple at Nippur, and Narâm-Sin, the son of Sargon, also calls himself the builder of Bêl's temple. Sargon's language, which we take from a door-socket found at Nippur, is: "Šargani-šar-âli, son of Itti-Bêl, the mighty king of Agade, builder of E-kur, temple of Bêl in Nippur".[1] The language of Narâm-Sin from a brick stamp found at Nippur is: "Narâm-Sin, builder of the temple of Bêl".[2] Neither Sargon nor his son meant that he was the original builder of E-kur. They were simply repairers of the temple, like many other kings. Many kings down to the last king of the last empire took much pride in rebuilding temples. There must have been a temple at Nippur when En-šag-kušanna presented the spoil of Kiš to Bêl. Excavations at Nippur show that, as there are great deposits of debris above the temple pavements made by Sargon and his son, so beneath these pavements there is a further great layer of debris, proving that the founding of E-kur must reach far back into the darkness of pre-historic antiquity. Sargon's bricks were the first to bear a stamp which we may consider to imply a date, but they were not the first bricks laid.

The *ziggurrat* which Ur-Gur, an early king of Ur, built is the first of which we have definite knowledge. We know something of the pavement that Sargon I. and Narâm-Sin built, but of the character of the buildings that might have rested on this pavement we have no information. Ur-Gur leveled the ground and built a new platform, 8 feet high and 100 by 170 feet in area with a *ziggurrat* consisting of three stages. Some of the facings of his structure were made of burnt brick, bearing the inscription of Ur-Gur (see N. II, 124). The greatest temple Nippur ever had was built by an Assyrian king; viz, Ašurbânipal. The structure covered a larger surface than any before it. The walls, instead of being plain, were ornamented with square half columns. The lower terrace was faced with baked brick, stamped with an inscription in which the *ziggurrat* is dedicated to Bêl, the lord of the lands, by Ašurbânipal, the mighty king, the king of the four quarters of the earth, the builder of E-kur (see N. II, 126).

E-kur, the temple of Bêl at Nippur, as restored on the basis of the discoveries of the University of Pennsylvania Exploration Fund, consists of two courts, an outer and an inner court. Within

---

[1] *ilu Šar-ga-ni-šar-âli mâr Itti-ilu Bêl da-num šàr A-ga-de-ki bân È-kur bît Bêl in Nippur-ki* (OBI No. 2).

[2] *ilu Naràm-ilu Sin bâni bît ilu Bêl* (OBI. 4).

the inner court stands the *ziggurrat*, rising to a tower of three or four stages which the most devout pilgrims might perhaps ascend. At the top is an enclosed shrine in which is a statue of Bêl. Here Bêl and his consort, Bêlit, for Babylonian gods maintain family relations like human beings, are supposed to dwell. In figurines Bêl appears as an old man, dressed in royal robes, generally carrying a thunder-bolt in his hand (see N. II, 128). By the side of the *ziggurrat* stands a temple for the use of the priests. We may assume on the whole, no doubt, that the assembly of pilgrims was confined chiefly to the outer court (see EBL. 470).

Bêl was at first a local deity, but as the circumference of the political territory of which Nippur was the religious centre was enlarged, so Bêl's cult was extended. Other cities included in the same political domain with Nippur, recognized Bêl as lord. Bêl was a sort of war god. Kings rivaled one another in courting his favor. The victorious king attributed his success to Bêl and brought the spoil to Bêl. The king of the south, whether of Lagaš, Erech or Ur, and the king of the north, whether of Kiš or Agade, always went to Nippur to celebrate his victory. In this way Bêl's lordship came to be recognized as extending over all Babylonia and finally over Assyria. Ḥammurabi, king at Babylon, 2300 B. C., recognized "Bêl as lord of heaven and earth, who determines the destiny of the land",[1] and Tiglath-pileser I (about 1100 B. C.), the first great Assyrian conqueror, called Bêl "the father of the gods and Bêl of the lands",[2] and speaks of himself as "appointed to dominion over the country of Bêl".[3]

The Semitic appropriation of En-lil involved some transformation in the conception of Bêl. Not to refer to Palestine, there were three Bêls; the Sumerian Bêl, the Semitic Bêl and the new Bêl or Marduk, who, however, was really a different god. The Babylonian Bêl, either in the mind of the Sumerian, of the Babylonian or of the Assyrian, always had his seat at Nippur.

Under Semitic influence Bêl became lord of the world. He was one in the hierarchy of three who ruled the universe; viz., Anu, the lord of the heavens, Bêl, the lord of the earth, and Ea, the lord of the deep. The Sumerian name, En-lil, made Bêl the "lord of fulness". The Semitic name Bêl emphasized the fact of his lordship, and the name of his temple, E-kur, "house of the mountain", marked out the scope of his lordship. The earth was conceived

---

[1] *ilu Bêl* (EN LIL) *be-el šá-me-e ù ir-ṣi-tim šá-i-im ši-ma-at mâtim* (KALAM) (Col. I, 3—7. See CH. Plate I).

[2] *ilu Bêl* (EN.LIL) *a-bu ilâni ilu Bêl* (EN) *mâtâte* (KUR.KUR) (I R. 9, Col. I, 3—4).

[3] (21b) *a-na šarru-ut* (22) *mât ilu Bêli* (EN.LIL) *rabi-eš tu-kin-na-šú* (I R. 9, Col. I).

of as a mountain resting on the abyss, and the temple with its *ziggurrat* was built to rise up like a mountain out of the deep. The people could stand in the court of the temple at Nippur and say of the mountain-like structure:

"O great mountain of Bêl, O airy mountain,
Whose summit reaches heaven,
Whose foundation in the shining deep is firmly laid,
On the land like a mighty bull lying,
With gleaming horns like the rays of the rising sun,
Like the stars of heaven that are filled with lustre!"[1]

When Babylon became the chief city of all Babylonia, it was natural that its god should be regarded as supreme. It was at this point that political lordship seemed to pass from the old Bêl to the new, namely to Marduk. Ḫammurabi, one of the early kings at Babylon, speaks of Bêl as voluntarily transferring his power to Marduk. In the Assyrian legend of the Creation this transfer is dramatically enacted. The task of overcoming the monster Tiâmat naturally belonged to Bêl. But Marduk, the youthful god of Eridu, the son of Ea, was urged to attempt the feat. When he had slain the monster, there was joy among the gods. They vied with each other in bestowing honor on the victor. Finally Bêl steps forward and confers an honor also. He bestowed on Marduk his own title with these words: "Father Bêl calls Marduk the lord of the world."[2] Marduk, therefore, is sometimes called the new Bêl in distinction from En-lil, the old Bêl.

The idea of origins is apparently not very fully elaborated in Babylonian literature. For instance, the Babylonians did not come so near to the idea of creation *ex nihilo* as the Hebrews. Their cosmogony starts with chaos. The expanse of the heavens appears specked with stars, some of which move with regularity. The moon travels across the expanse according to a prescribed order. Then the Babylonian bilingual account of the Creation gives a short statement of the creation of the land and sea, of man and beast. Generally, however, the divinity that planned and perfected order seems to be far in the background. The bilingual account says:

"Marduk constructed an enclosure before the waters,
He made dust and heaped it up within the enclosure.

---

[1] (15) *kur-gal* *dingir* *En-lil-lá im-ḫar-sag gú-bi an da-ab-di-a zu-ab azag-ga-bi* (16) *suḫ-bi uš-uš-e apin-apin-e* (19) *kur-kur-ra ama ban-da ba-da nà-a-dim* (21) *si še-ir-zi si* *dingir* *Babbar mul-mul-la-dim* (23) *mul an-na dil-bad-du i-si-iš lal-a-dim* (K. 4898. IV R. 27, No. 2).

[2] *be-el mâtâte* (KUR KUR) *šumi*(MU)-*šu it-ta-bi a-bi* *ilu* *Bêl* (EN.LIL) (K. 8522 Rev. 13. CT. XIII. Plate 27).

Mankind he created.
Animals of the field, creatures of the field he created.
The Tigris and the Euphrates he made and in place put (them)
By their names joyfully he called them".[1]

Now Marduk, we know, took the place of Bêl and Bêl handed over his prerogatives to Marduk. In transferring his rights he must have given over also his power to create. If Marduk possessed the power to create in the time of his popularity, Bêl must have had the same power in the days of his glory, before he was succeeded by Marduk. Therefore we are led to the belief that the early Babylonians looked upon Bêl as the creator of animal and human life on earth.

The following hymn may be regarded as embodying a legendary view of Bêl as creator, while the idea of destruction is also incorporated in the hymn:

"Of Bêl, mighty hand,
Who lifts up glory and splendour, day of power
Fearfulness he establishes.
Lord of DUN.PA.UD.DU.A, mighty hand.
Fearfulness he establishes.
Stormy one, father, mother, creator, mighty hand.
The catch-net he throws over the hostile land.
Lord, great warrior, mighty hand.
A firm house he raises up; the enemy he overthrows.
The shining one, lord of Nippur, mighty hand.
The lord, the life of the land, the *massû* of heaven and earth."[2]

2. *Sin*

Next after Bêl, the moon-god is worthy of consideration, because of the age of his cult, and because of the greatness of its influence in Babylonia. The moon-god had two Sumerian names,

---

[1] (17) . . . *gi-ši-ma gi-dir i-de-na-a nam-mi-ni-in-kešda* ilu *Marduk a-ma-am ina pa-an me-e ir-ku-us* (18) *saḫar-ra ni-mù-a ki a-dag nam-mi-in-dub e-pi-ri ib-ni-ma it-ti a-mi iš-pu-uk* (20) *nam-lù-gišgal-lu ba-ru a-me-lu-ti ib-ta-ni* (22) *bir-anšu nig-zi-gal edin-na ba-ru bu-ul ṣêri ši-kin na-piš-ti ina ṣi-e-ri ib-ta-ni* (23) *ìd Idigna ìd Puranunu me-dim ki gar-ra-dim Diglat ù Puratta ib-ni-ma ina aš-ri iš-ku-un* (24) *mu-ne-ne-a nam-duga mi-ni-in-sá-a šum-ši-na ṭa-biš im-bi* (Tablet 82—5—22, 1048. CT. XIII. Plate 36).

[2] (47) *dimmer Mu-ul-lil-lá-ra id-kal* (48) *su-zi me-lam gur-ru ud al-tar* (49) *im-ḫuš ri-a-bi* (52) *u dimmer* DUN.PA.UD DU.A-*ra id-kal* (53) *nam-tar gu-la im-ḫuš ri-a-bi* (56) *mu-lu lil a-a damal muḫ-na id-kal* (58) *sa-šú-uš-gal ki bal-a šu-šu* (60) *u ur-sag gal-e id-kal* (61) *è gi gur-ru mulu êrim-ma šu-šu* (62) *azag gašan En-lil-ki-a-ra id-kal* (63) *am ši ka-nag-gà maš-su ki-in-gi-ra* (K. 4980. IV R. 27, No. 4).

two Assyrian names and two great temples. The Sumerian name most often applied to the moon-god is Šis-ki, the particular meaning of which in this case does not seem to be very patent. If the two syllables *Šis* and *ki* are taken as nouns, the one is the construct state and the other in the genitive relation; the name means "brother of the land", that is, "protector of the land", or "helper of the land". The other Sumerian name is En-zu, lord of wisdom, the intellectual attribute of wisdom being closely related to the physical property of giving light. While therefore Šis-ki expresses the material relation of the moon to the earth, En-zu seems to state the intellectual relation of the moon-god to the affairs of the earth. The first Assyrian name of the moon-god to be considered is Nannar. The derivation of this name is still in doubt. It generally occurs in bilingual literature as the Assyrian equivalent of the Sumerian Šis-ki (see IV R. 9, 3—18). Jastrow thinks that the word Nannar is made by the reduplication of *nar*, "light", and the assimilation of the first *r*, Nar + nar = Nannar (see RBA. p. 72). The other Assyrian name, connected with the moon-god more often at Harran than at Ur, is Sin, the sign being EŠ, used also for "thirty", and is applied to the moon-god as the deity of the month of thirty days. As the cult of the moon-god traveled from Ur to Harran, so the name of Sin traveled even into the peninsula of Arabia and probably became a local name there in the wilderness. The Assyrian kings of the second empire seemed to prefer to call the moon-god by the name Sin, but the Semitic Babylonians called him Nannar.

Nannar had a temple at Ur, called E-gišširgal, and one at Harran, known as E-ḫulḫul. Ur was the oldest of the two temple cities. Its history may possibly reach back to 4000 B. C. Ur held a position in southern Babylonia similar to that held by Nippur in northern Babylonia, but was not so old as Nippur. Ur was the religious centre in the south with Nannar as the state god, as Nippur was the religious centre in the north with Bêl as the state god. When the states of the south and the north were united under Ḫammurabi, Babylon, becoming the religious capital of the south and the north combined, the state lustre of the god of Babylon naturally came to dim the glory of the god of Ur as well as that of Nippur. Harran, situated on the Euphrates in the northern part of Assyria, never figured in state power, and was prominent only because of the importance of the events that centered there, on the road between the east and the west.

Nabonidus, the last Semitic Babylonian king (555—538 B. C.) was an enthusiastic devotee of the moon-god. He tells us what Ašurbânipal did to the temple of the moon-god at Mugheir. In speaking of that temple, he calls it the house of Sin which Ašurbânipal, king of Assyria, son of Esarhaddon, king of Assyria had built. Nabonidus himself rebuilt both the temples of the moon-god, the temple of E-gišširgal at Ur and the temple of E-ḫulhul at Harran, and he gives us a description of the rebuilding of both. We also have two prayers of Nabonidus addressed to the moon-god, one addressed to him at E-gišširgal, the other addressed to him at E-ḫulḫul (see I R. 68, Col. I, 6 ff. and V R 64, Col. I, 8 ff.).

The temple ruins of E-gišširgal have been well uncovered. The temple is of rectangular form, the four corners turned towards the four cardinal points of the compass. The platform of the base is at the level of the roofs of the houses, made of solid masonry of bricks and reached by steps at the end. On the platform are two stagings, also of solid masonry reached by steps at one end. On the second staging is a shrine of the moon-god. In sculpture he appears as an old man with long beard and dressed in royal robes. He wears a hat and in the scene there is always a thin crescent (see Clercq, Vol. I, Plates X—XV). Loftus and Taylor both give drawings of the temple of E-gišširgal (see TR. p. 127 and JRAS. XV, p. 260) The ruins of the temple of the moon-god at Harran have not yet been uncovered to the extent that the plan of the temple can be laid before us.

Theologically, Nannar stood at the head of the second triad of gods. The hierarchy of the universe consisted of the god Anu, the god Bêl and the god Ea. The hierarchy of heaven consisted of the god Nannar, the god Šamaš and the god Ištar; that is, the moon-god, the sun-god and the star-god. The reason for placing Nannar above Šamaš was that Nannar was the god of the ruling city, while Šamaš was the city god of the dependent state, though the sun which Šamaš represents is stronger than the moon which Nannar represents, and we should expect Šamaš, therefore, to receive the first place. The god of the city of Larsa was Šamaš. The god of the city of Ur was Nannar. When Larsa became subject to Ur, the god of Larsa; viz., Šamaš, became the child of the god of Ur; that is, of Nannar. The relation of the night to the calendar also shows that the rank of Nannar was superior to that of Šamaš. The day began at evening; not with the morning. The sun too was the son of the night; that is, it issued forth from the night, in the morning. Kings, thinking of this fact, that the sun was born of the night, often addressed Šamaš as the offspring of the god Sin. The rising of the moon in the night to send forth its light into the darkness also impressed the Babylonian with the power of the moon. The waxing and waning of the moon left the same impression on the Babylonian mind. The regularity of the phases of the moon and its effect upon the tides as well showed the moon to be an agent in marking time. Finally, the place of the moon among the stars also gave him the appearance of having royal sway.

Nannar's national influence was much like that of Bêl. Geographically, he represented southern Babylonia, while Bêl was the chief deity of northern Babylonia. When Marduk became the patron god of Babylon, Bêl and Nannar still held their positions as patron gods, but in subordination to Marduk. Besides, they did not lose their influence as supreme deities, each in his peculiar sphere, Bêl as the god of the earth and Nannar as the god of the moon. Bêl was ruler of the earth while Nannar was, by his light, a producer in the earth. Bêl was the providential director of life on earth, Nannar was the originator of life on earth, as he formed the child in the womb. Both were superhuman in power and wisdom. Thus Ḫammurabi: "My words are mighty. If a man pay no attention to my words, may Bêl, the lord who determines destinies, whose command cannot be altered, who has enlarged my dominion, drive him out from his dwelling. May Sin, the lord of heaven, my divine creator, whose scimetar shines among the gods, take away from him the crown and throne of sovereignty."[1]

No god in the mind of the Babylonian had reached the position of combining in himself all the qualities of divinity. So it did not seem inconsistent to the Babylonian to worship two gods like Bêl and Nannar, or more gods. There was a tolerance of all gods; each was considered as acting in his own circle, and these circles did not necessarily exclude the one the other. One god might be more important than another, according to the importance of the circle in which his virtue was effective, or according to the importance of the political power the circle of whose sway was under the special tutelage of some particular god. Babylonian worship cannot be said to be polytheistic in the grosser form, nor had it reached the higher ideal that lies in monotheism. It may properly be considered a henotheistic worship in which there is a pantheon of gods whose local and universal claims did not cause the gods or their devotees to war the one on the other.

There is a truly great bilingual hymn addressed to Nannar. According to the colophon it was transcribed by the chief penman of Ašurbânipal from an old copy. My impression is that it is an

---

[1] (Col. XLI, 99) *a-mâ*(PI)-*tu-ú-a na-aš-ga* (Col. XLII, 18) *šum-ma a-mè*(PI)-*lum* (19) *a-mâ*(PI)-*ti-ia* (22) *la i-gul--ma* (53) *ilu Bêl* (EN.LIL) *belum* (54) *mu-ši-im ši-ma-tim* (55) *šá ki-bè*(NE)-*zu* (56) *la ut-ta-ka-ru* (57) *mušar-bu-ù* (58) *šar-ru-ti-ia* (62) *i-na šú-ub-ti-šú* (63) *li-šá-ab-bi-ḫa-aš-šum* (Col. XLIII, 41) *ilu Sin* (EN.ZU) *be-el šá-me-e* (42) *ilum*(AN) *ba-ni-i* (43) *šá še-ri-zu* (44) *i-na ili*(NI.NI) *šú-pa-a-al* (45) *agâm kussâm šá šar-rutim* (46) *li-te-ir-šú* (CḪ. Plates LXXVI, LXXVII and LXXIX).

enlargement of the hymn to Nannar of which this Thesis gives a transliteration, translation and commentary. For this reason I herewith append the following translation:

"O lord, highest of the gods, alone in heaven and earth exalted!
O father Nannar, lord of Anšar, highest of the gods!
O father Nannar, lord Anu the great, highest of the gods!
O father Nannar, lord Sin, highest of the gods!
O father Nannar, lord of Ur, highest of the gods!
O father Nannar, lord of E-gišširgal, highest of the gods!
O father Nannar, lord of the shining crown, highest of the gods!
O father Nannar, of most perfect royalty, highest of the gods!
O father Nannar, in royal robes marching, highest of the gods!
O strong young bullock, with great horns, of perfect physical strength, with hazel-colored pointed beard of luxurious growth and perfect fulness!
'O fruit, whose stalk growing of itself reacheth a tall form, beautiful to look upon, whose perfection never satiateth!
O mother, the producer of life, thou who settest up for the creatures of life a lofty dwelling!
O merciful and gracious father, thou who holdest in hand the life of all the land!
O lord, thy divinity, like the distant heavens and the broad sea, inspireth reverence!
O creator of the lands, founding the temple and giving it a name!
O namer of royalty, determiner of the future for distant days!
O mighty prince, whose distant thought no god can declare.
O thou whose knee bendeth not, opener of the road for the gods thy brothers!
O thou who goest forth from the foundation of heaven to the height of heaven, opening the door of heaven, creating light for all men!
O father, begetter of all, who lookest upon the creatures of life, who thinkest of them!
O lord, who fixest the destiny of heaven and earth, whose command no one changeth!
O thou who holdest the fire and the water, who turnest the life of creation, what god reacheth thy fulness!
Who in heaven is high? Thou alone art high.
Who on earth is high? Thou alone art high.
As for thee, when thy word is spoken in heaven, the Igigi bow down the face.
As for thee, when thy word is spoken on earth, the Anunaki kiss the ground.
As for thee, when thy word like the wind resoundeth on high, food and drink abound.

As for thee, when thy word is established in the land, it causeth vegetation to grow.
As for thee, thy word maketh fat the herd and flock and inceaseth the creatures of life.
As for thee, thy word secureth truth and righteousness and causeth men to speak righteousness.
As for thee, thy word extendeth to heaven, it covereth the earth, no one can comprehend it.
As for thee, thy word, who can understand it, who can approach it!
O lord, in heaven supreme, on earth the leader, among the gods thy brothers without a rival.
O king of kings, the lofty one, whose command no one approacheth, whose divinity no god can liken.
Where thy eye looketh thou showest favor, where thy hand toucheth thou securest salvation.
O lord, the shining one, who directeth truth and righteousness in heaven and earth and causeth them to go forth.
Look graciously on thy temple, look graciously on thy city.
Look graciously on Ur, look graciously on E-gišširgal,
Thy beloved consort, the gracious mother, calleth to thee: O lord give rest!
The hero Šamaš calleth to thee: O lord give rest!
The Igigi call to thee: O lord give rest!
The Anunnaki call to thee: O lord give rest!
. . . . . calleth to thee: O lord give rest!
Ningal calleth to thee: O lord give rest!
May the bar of Ur, the enclosure of E-gišširgal and the building of Ezida be established!
The gods of heaven and earth call to thee: O lord give rest!
The lifting up of the hand. 48 lines on the tablet to Nannar.
Mighty one. Lord of strength.
Like its original, copied and revised.
Tablet of Ištar-šuma-ereš, the chief scribe.
Of Ašurbânipal, king of legions, king of Assyria,
Son of Nabu-zer-lištešir, chief penman." IV R. 9.

This Ašurbânipal hymn may be considered as remarkable for its advanced ideas. In the first part of the hymn there is introduced the mythological idea of the bullock's head in the moon with horns and the face with flowing hazel-colored beard, so that strength and brilliancy are pointed out. But the hymn advances into literal speech by which the most varied and greatest of divine attributes are attached to the god Nannar. He is named as sovereign god, a self-created god, a merciful god, the begetter of all life, the maintainer of the life of the world, the bestower of gifts to men, the establisher of dwellings; he fixes destinies, pronounces judgment, gives water to man and supplies him with vegetable food. He holds a unique and exalted position in heaven and on earth above all other beings. To him the angels of heaven and spirits of earth bow, and at his command the forces of nature perform their marvellous functions.

3. *Adad*

The storm-god is known by the Sumerian ideogram *Im*. The sign IMMU in the El-Amarna tablets (1500 B. C.) has the reading Adad, a name connected with the Syrian Hadad. Oppert thinks Adad is the god's oldest name. It seems evidently a foreign equivalent for *Im*. The Assyrian name Ramman is a provisional name meaning "thunderer", and probably only an epithet. The sign IMMU has also the value *Mer*. This is, no doubt, the original and real name of the god, which appears as well in the form Immer. The primary idea in the name is that of wind, then, that of rain and finally of thunder and lightning. The god is not an object like Nannar, but a force; then the force is personified and he is spoken of as a person. Ḥammurabi puts him in the second triad of gods. He is the third person of that triad, Sin being the first person and Šamaš the second. Generally Ištar has the third place in the second triad. In that case Ramman falls outside of that triad and takes position among all the gods as seventh in importance. The order is as follows: Anu, Bêl, Ea, Sin, Šamaš, Ištar, Adad (Ramman). As a Babylonian god we find Ramman's name appears in Ḥammurabi's time as a common name in literature. He is invoked in Ḥammurabi's Code, like other gods, of course in his sphere as a storm-god. Thus: "If a man will pay no attention to my words, may Adad, the lord of abundance, the regent of heaven and earth, my helper, deprive him of the rain from heaven and the water-floods from the springs! May he bring his land to destruction through want and hunger! May he break loose furiously over his city and turn his land into a heap left by a whirlwind!"[1] With the kings of the Cassite dynasty Ramman seems to be popular. His name appears by the side of that of Šamaš and he is called the divine lord of justice. In the Babylonian dynasty of kings, Nebuchadnezzar I. addresses Ramman as the great lord of heaven, the lord of the subterranean waters and rain, whose curse is invoked against the one who sets aside the decrees of Nebuchadnezzar or defaces his monument.

---

[1] (Col. XLII, 18a) *šum-ma a-mè*(PI)*-lum* (19) *a-mâ*(PI)*-ti-ia* (22) *la i-gul-ma* (Col XLIII, 64) *ilu Adad be-el ḫêgallim* (65) *gu-gal šá-me-e* (66) *ù ir-ṣi-tim* (67) *ri-zu-ú-a* (68) *zu-ni i-na šá-me-e* (69) *mi-lam* (70) *i-na na-aḳ-bi-im* (71) *li-te-ir-šú* (72) *ma-zu* (73) *i-na ḫu-šá-aḫ-ḫi-im* (74) *ù bu-bu-tim* (75) *li-ḫal-li-iḳ* (76) *e-li ali-šú* (77) *iz-zi-iš* (78) *li-is-si-ma* (79) *ma-zu a-na til a-bu-bi-im* (80) *li-te-ir* (CḤ. Plates LXXVI, LXXIX and LXXX).

Ramman is thought to be more truly an Assyrian than a Babylonian god. He is almost as dear to the Assyrian as the god Ašur. Historical data, however, do not furnish very early mention of his name in Assyria. We find that he had a seat of worship in Damascus, and his cult had vogue in the plain of Jezreel, his name appearing in Hebrew, written by mistake, after the text was Masoretically vocalized, "Rimmon" which is exactly the same in form as the Hebrew word for pomegranate. In Assyria we can trace his history back to some extent by means of inscriptions in which his name appears as an element in the compound names of kings. For example, we find his name in the name of the ancient Assyrian king Šamaš-Ramman, and from an inscription of Tiglath-pileser I. we learn also that Šamaš-Ramman built a temple to the god Ramman. So we have historical evidence that the cult of Ramman is older in Assyria than this king, who was reigning in 1820 B. C. How much older it may be we do not know. Jastrow thinks that the cult is indigenous to Assyrian soil.

Between the time of Šamaš-Ramman and the time of Tiglath-pileser I. the service of Ramman must have declined somewhat, for the temple of Ramman in the city of Aššur seems not to have been repaired from the days of Šamaš-Ramman till Tiglath-pileser himself rebuilt it. Tiglath-pileser says that from the time of the founding it was in decay six hundred and forty years. Then king Ašurdan tore it down entirely. Sixty years after the entire destruction, Tiglath-pileser builds the temple anew. He says that in the beginning of his government the great gods Anu and Adad demanded for him the restoration of their sacred dwelling. "I made bricks and cleared its ground until I reached the artificial flat terrace upon which the old temple had been built. I laid its foundation upon the solid rock and the whole place incased with bricks like a fire-place, overlaid on it a layer of fifty bricks in depth and built upon this the foundations of the temple of Anu and Adad of large square stones. I built it up from foundation to roof, larger and grander than before, and erected also two great temple towers . . . . . fitting ornaments of their great divinities."[1] From Tiglath-pileser on, temples of Ramman do not seem to be often mentioned, but the god himself is frequently spoken of in inscriptions of the kings. Sargon II. has one of the eastern gates

[1] (Col. VII, 75b) *libnâti al-bi-in* (76) *ḥaḫ-ḥar-šu ú-mi-si* (77) *dan-na-su ak-šud uš-še-e-šú* (78) *i-na eli ki-ṣir šadi-i dan-ni ad-di* (79) *aš-ra šá-a-tu a-na si-ḫir-ti-šú* (80) *i-na libnâti ki-ma ka-nu-ni aš-pu-uk* (81) *L ti-ip-ki a-na šú-pa-li* (82) *ú-ṭi-bi i-na muḫ-ḫi-šú* (83) *uš-še bit ilu A-nim ù ilu Ramman* (84) *šá bu-u-li ad-di* (85) *iš-tu uš-še-šú a-di taḫ-lu-bi-šú* (86) *e-bu-uš eli maḫ-ri-e ut-tir* (87) II *si-ḫur-ra-te rabu-te* (88) *šá a-na si-mat ilu-ti-šú-nu rabi-te* (89) *šú-lu-ka lu-ú ab-ni-ma* (I R 15).

of his temple named "Ramman the producer of abundance". Ašurbânipal enumerates thirteen gods whom he honors as the great gods, and places Ramman fifth in the list.

Ramman's most esteemed service was that of bestowing blessing The rains in the right proportion were a boon to the land, filling the canals and watering the soil. Ḫammurabi calls Ramman the lord of abundance and his helper. Tiglath-pileser I. prays for the blessings of prosperity, as he prays to Adad: "May Anu and Adad turn to me truly and accept graciously the lifting up of my hand, hearken unto my devout prayers, grant me and my reign abundance of rain, years of prosperity and fruitfulness in plenty."[1] Ašurbânipal describes the blessings he receives by the favor of this god: "Ramman let loose his showers and Ea has opened his springs, the grain has grown to a height of five yards and the ears have been five sixths of a yard long, the produce of the land has been abundant and the fruit trees have borne fruit richly."[2] The mention of Anu and Ea with Ramman is because of their power to produce water, Ea representing the depths of water and Anu the heaven with its clouds of rain

The most conspicuous work of Ramman was that of destruction. It is in this function of judgment that he is associated with Šamaš. The connection lies in the fact that the lightning of Ramman is like the day-light of Šamaš; so, as the god of lightning, Ramman has the title *birḳu.* Lightning and flooding rain were, because of their destructive character, fearful forces, and the kings in calling for a curse on hostile man or land turn to Ramman in imprecation, as, for example, Raman-Nirari I. does concerning the man who may be tempted to blot out the record of Ramman-Nirari's name: "May Ramman with terrible rainstorm overwhelm him, may flood, destruction, wind, rebellion, revolution, tempest, want and famine, drought and hunger be continually in his land. May he come down on his land like a flood. May he turn it into mounds and ruins. May Ramman strike his land with a destructive bolt."[3]

---

[1] (Col. VIII, 23) *ilu A-nim ù ilu Rammânu* (24) *ki-niš li-siḫ-ru-ni-ma* (25) *ni-iš ḳa-ti-ia li-ra-mu* (26) *te-me-iḳ ik-ri-be-ia liš-me-ú* (27) *zu-ú-ni da-aḫ-du-te šá-na-at* (28) *nu-uḫ-še ù bar-ri-e a-na pali-ia* (29) *liš-ru-ku* (I R. 16)

[2] (Col. I, 45) *ilu Rammânu zunni-šu ú-maš-ši-ra ilu È-a û-paṭ-ṭi-ra naḳbu-šu* (46) *ḫanšu ana ammatu še-am iš-ḳu ina abšeni-šu* (47) *e-ri-ik šú-bul-tu parab ana ammatu* (48 a) *išir eburu* (50) *šú-um-mu-ḫa in-bu* (V R. 1).

[3] (38 b) *ilu Rammânu i-na ri-ḫi-iṣ* (39) *li-mu-ti li-ir-ḫi-su a-bu-bu* (40) *šaru limnu sa-aḫ-ma-aš-tu te-šú-ú* (41) *a-šam-šú-tu su-un-ḳu bu-bu-tu* (42) *a-ru-ur-tu ḫu-šá-ḫu i-na mâti-šú lu ka-ia-an mâti-šu a-bu-bi-iš lu-uš-ba-i* (43) *a-na tili u kar-mi lu-ti-ir ilu Rammânu i-na be-ri-šú li-mu-ti mâti-šu li-ib-ri* (IV R. 39, Rev.).

Some Babylonian composer has set forth the terrifying side of Ramman's character in a bilingual hymn as follows:

"The lord in his anger himself makes heaven quake.
Adad in his wrath lifts up the earth.
The mighty mountain he himself smites down.
At his anger, at his wrath,
At his roaring, at his thundering,
The gods of heaven ascend to heaven,
The gods of earth enter earth,
Šamaš into the foundation of heaven enters,
Sin in the height of heaven is magnified."[1]

4. *Tammuz*

There is a fascination about the life of Tammuz not experienced in the contemplation of the other gods of Babylonia. He seems to be presented to us just as though he were a man.

Our first paragraph may describe him as a resident of one of the ancient cities of southern Babylonia. The city of his residence was Eridu on the banks of the Euphrates. His official title is that of sun-god and his occupation is to care for the growth of plants. The name of his father was Ea, the lord of the city of Eridu, whose duties consisted in governing the waters of the river on whose shore the city rested. Tammuz had a mother, whose name was Davkina, the mistress of the vine. Tammuz also had a sister Belili whose calling was, like that of Tammuz her brother, the care of plant growth. Tammuz also had a bride, the famous and treacherous Ištar, the goddess of love, represented by the evening star; she was mistress of the neighbouring city of Erech, a little to the north-west, and on the other side of the Euphrates. The life of Tammuz at Eridu was romantic and his days ended in tragedy. There is a little poem, giving a picture of his home. There was a garden, a holy place, abundantly shaded with profuse leafage of trees whose roots went down deep into the waters over which Ea presided. His couch was hung under the rich foliage of the vine which his mother tended. There Tammuz dwelt and

[1] (9b) *an mu-un-da-ùr-ùr* (10) *be-lum ina a-ga-gi-šu ša-mu-ú i-ta-na-ar-ra-ru-šú* (11) *dimmer Mer šur-ra-na ki ši-in-ga-bul-bul* (12) *ilu Rammânu ina e-zi-zi-šu ir-ṣi-tum i-na-as-su* (13) *ḫar-sag gal-gal-e šà-ka-a ba-an-na-ḳu-eš* (14) *ša-du-ú ra-bu-tu su-uḫ-ḫu-pu-šu* (15) *ib-ba-bi-ta šur-ra-bi-ta* (16) *a-na a-ga-gi-šu a-na e-zi-zi-šu* (17) (?)*-ge-bi-ta ḫar-du-bi-ta* (18) *a-na šá-gi-mi-šu a-na ra-mi-mi-šu* (19) *dim-me-ir an-na-ge an-na ba-an-dul-du-ne* (20) *ilâni ša ša-me-e a-na šam-e i-te-lu-u* (21) *dim-me-ir ki-ge ki-a ba-an-búl-ne-eš* (22) *ilâni ša ir-ṣi tim a-na ir-ṣi-tim i-te-ir-bu* (23) *dimmer Babbar an úr-ra ba-da-šu-šu-ru* (24) *ina i-šid šame-e i-te-ru-ub* (25) *dimmer Siš-ki an pa-šù ba-da-kabar* (26) *ina e-lat šame-e ir-ta-bi* (IV R. 28, 2).

there was his shrine. His dwelling of foliage in his youthful days was symbolic of the domain in which the virtue of his power was to be exercised. His real home was in heaven, for from heaven the virtue of plant-growth procedes with the heat of the sun. But his connection with heaven had been forgotten, except in reminiscence found in legend. In the legend of Adapa, for instance, we find a hint of it. Tammuz and his companion Gišzida are seen mounting up to heaven where they receive stations as door-keepers in the gate of Anu's house; in heaven they properly belong.

The descent of Tammuz to the lower world implies that he died, but the accounts have not made a direct statement of how he died, or what was the cause of his death Perhaps we may conceive of the event of his death as having taken place at Eridu before the service of lamentation had developed into a cult honored at the court of Sargon of Akkad, where a temple was built for Tammuz after northern Babylonia had gained the ascendency over southern Babylonia. The literal cause of his death was that he was not capable of making plant-growth a continuous process. The power of the heat of the sun as the summer advanced was superior to the virtue which Tammuz possessed over plant-life. The fierce heat of the summer caused vegetation to take a paler hue; then the germs of decay entered; slowly and surely the face of the land was assuming the same state that existed before the power of Tammuz appeared to quicken the blade of grass and the fruit-bud of the early spring. So Tammuz was banished to the lower world. Romantically his entrance to the abode of the dead was due to the hand which Ištar had in the events of his life. She had many lovers, and she betrayed them all. Her betrayal in the case of Tammuz consisted in not aiding him in her sphere as great mother in the production of life on earth. Had she supplemented his effort and made the earth continue to bear and bring forth, counteracting the effect of the deadly heat of the summer solstice and the destructive wind of the south, the gardens and the fruit orchards over whose productiveness Tammuz presided would have enjoyed perennial fruitage, and Gilgameš would never have had to take up the sad accusation against Ištar:

"Tammuz, the spouse of thy youth,
Thou compellest to weep year after year."[1]

Also there had never gone up the song of lamentation:

"He went down to meet the nether world,
He has sated himself, Šamaš caused him to perish
To the land of the dead.

[1] (46) *a-na* *ilu* *Dumu-zi ḫa-mi-ri ṣu-*[*uḫ-*]*ri-ti-ki* (47) *šat-ta a-na šat-ti bi-tak-ka-a tal-ti-miš-šu* (BN. Tafel VI).

With mourning was he filled on the day
When he fell into great sorrow."[1]

According to another story of the fate of Tammuz, Ištar was the victim of sudden and violent passion, and in a fit of anger for disregard of her command she had smitten him down, just as she crushed the *allallu*-bird she loved:

"Thou didst crush him and break his pinions.
In the woods he stands and laments,
'O my pinions'."[2]

Also as she cast out of her sight the lion:

"Thou didst love a lion of perfect strength,
Seven and seven times thou didst bury him in the corners."[3]

The origin of the service of weeping for Tammuz is an interesting legend. When Ištar had slain her lover, she hastened, like the going down of the evening star, to the lower world in search of waters to restore him to life. She searches long, passing through all the compartments of Hades. The story does not give details of her finding Tammuz, but instead, a scene of his burial is introduced:

"To Tammuz, her youthful consort
Pour out pure waters, costly oil."[4]

A scene of the mourning for Tammuz is also introduced, which may be taken as the original lamentation, all other summer solstice weepings being anniversaries of this original one. His sister is there lamenting:

"O my only brother, let me not perish!"[5]

And a great company of mourners sing dirges by the accompanyment of the flute and follow the instruction which Tammuz, though dead, seems to be giving then and there:

"On the day of Tammuz play for me,
On the flute of *uknu* and *samtu*!
With it play for me! With it play for me!

---

[1] (23) *il-lak i-lak ana i-rat ir-ṣi-tim* (25) *uš-ta-bar-ri* *ilu* *Šamaš ir-ta-bi-šu ana ir-ṣi-tim mi-tu-ti* (27) *ni-iz-za-tu ma-li i-na û-um im-ḳu-tu-ma ina i-dir-tim* (IV R. 30, 2).

[2] (49) *tam-ḫa-ṣi-šú-ma kap-pa-šú tal-te-bir* (50) *iz-za-az ina ḳi-ša-tim i-šis-si kap-pi* (BN. Tafel-VI).

[3] (51) *ta-ra-mi-ma nêšu ga-mi-ir e-mu-ki* (52) 7 *u* 7 *tu-uḫ-tar-ri-iš-šu šú-ut-ta-a-ti* (BN. Tafel VI).

[4] (47) *a-na* *ilu* *Dumu-zi ḫa-mir ṣi-iḫ-ru-ti-ša* (48) *mê il-lu-ti ra-am-me-ik šamnu ṭâbu* (from Ištar's Descent into Hades. K. 162. Reverse. CT. XV, Plate 47. Also IV R. 31).

[5] (55) *a-ḫi e-du la ta-ḫab-bil-an-ni* (from Ištar's Descent into Hades. K. 162. Reverse. CT. XV, Plate 47. Also IV R. 31).

O male and female mourners!
That the dead may arise and inhale incense!"[1]

Of course the story is not finished and the circle of events not completed without the resurrection of Tammuz. In a Chaldaean intaglio there is a picture of Tammuz rejuvenated on the knees of Ištar (see Clercq Vol. I, Plate IX, No. 83). Some forms of the story must include his return to the earth, and the complete service of lamentation must have been sometimes supplemented by a service of joy in which the idea of resurrection was significant.

Though the original lamentation was an expression of grief for Tammuz dead, the fully developed ceremony was an expression of several pathetic ideas. It was accompanied with sacrifice and offerings of wine. In Babylonia the commemoration was observed every year on the second day of the fourth month, called the month of Tammuz. It was not only a weeping for dead Tammuz, but a weeping for dead vegetation. The dying leaf had a mourner. The withered stock had a sympathizing friend. For the blasted blade of grass there was shed a tear. For the barren tree bereft of golden foliage and luscious fruit there went up a cry of sympathy. The ceremony was an expression of sadness that came over the people as the oppression of the heat of summer bore down upon them, the water supply being reduced, vegetable life put out and human life consequently made almost unendurable by the deprivation and heat of summer. The time of weeping was one for the expression of personal sorrow that lurks in almost every heart. The wail of anguish was a relief to souls burdened with their own peculiar griefs. The soul found relief in lifting up the voice attuned to some form of elegy. There came a relief like the rolling of the burden of guilt from the breast. The ceremony was one that embraced in its performance the expression of confession. It was, however, performed with the consciousness that the drought of summer was but for a season, and that there was to follow a period of happier existence, as the succeeding winter should merge into a new spring.

Tammuz was supposed to leave the land with the season when the spring growth was completed, to come back again in the following year. He is considered as dead, but his death is not an absolute one. He tells the mourners what to do as they gather about his bier. According to some allusions he seems also to be a lord, as it were, in the bowels of the earth, preparing the inner earth for putting forth a new stock of vegetation, as spring shall come. Hence, the hymn to Tammuz in this Thesis calls him

[1] (56) *ina û-me* *ilu* *Dumu-zi el-la-an-ni malil* *abnu* *uḳni* *abnu* *sâmti it-ti-šu el-la-an-ni* (57) *it-ti-šu el-la-an-ni* *amelu* ÊR (A.ŠI) *pl.* *u zinništu* ÊR (A.ŠI) *pl.* A.ŠI (58) *mituti li-lu-nim-ma ḳuṭ-ri-in li-iṣ-ṣi-nu* (from Ištar's Descent into Hades. K. 162. Reverse. CT. XV, Plate 47. Also IV R. 31).

"the generator of the lower world". His association with his friend Giššida substantiates more fully the idea of his resurrection. To give vitality to his work he still maintains his old personality of sun-god, and to him again is given a seat in heaven, as the Adapa legend shows:

"On mounting up to heaven,
At the gate of Anu
Tammuz and Giššida were stationed."[1]

The story of Tammuz seems to have taken deep and almost universal hold of the imagination and sympathy of mankind. The weeping for Tammuz is said to have been maintained by the Babylonians till a very late period. Similar stories to that of the Tammuz legend existed in about the same period of history among the Phoenicians, the Hebrews, the Greeks and the Egyptians, the most of these accounts having a common origin; if they have more than one origin, they seem nevertheless to blend in the main into one story. It is said that in the Phoenician town of Gebal by the Mediterranian on the road leading from the people of the east to those of the west, there is a yearly lamentation over the death of their sun-god, the beloved Aštoreth, who had been slain by a cruel hand, just as the spring verdure was cut down by the hot blasts of summer. The women, tearing their hair, disfiguring their faces and cutting their breasts, sent up a cry to heaven· "O my brother!" Across the sea by the way of Cyprus, the cry is said to have been carried to Greece where it found embodiment in the story of Adonis and Aphrodite. Possibly, however, the Greek story may be indigenous. Adonis lost his life while hunting, thrust through the thigh with the tusk of a wild boar. After death he was in great favour with Persephone who finally yielded to the entreaties of the inconsolable Aphrodite, and Adonis spent one half of the year with his celestial mistress and the other half with his infernal one. How much place the annual weeping for a departed one had among the Hebrews may be inferred to some extent by the mention made in the Scriptures of the service. Zechariah speaks of the well-known mourning of Hadadrimmon in the valley of Megiddon, and Amos refers to the custom of mourning for an only son. Ezekiel says that the Lord brought him to Jehovah's house "and behold, there sat the women weeping for Tammuz". Jeremiah goes a step further and gives us the refrain which was used in the weeping: "Ah me! Ah my brother!" The parallel story in Egypt had for its hero the god Osiris who, representing goodness, upon being slain by a foe, became judge of the dead, though his soul continued in existence among men.

---

[1] (2) *a-na ša-me-e i-na e-li-šú a-na ba-ab* *ilu* *A-ni i-na țe-ḫe-šú* (3) *i-na ba-a-bu* *ilu* *A-ni* *ilu* *Dumu-zi* *ilu* *Giš-zi-da iz-za-az-zu* (from the Legend of Adapa and the South Wind. TEA. Vol. III, 240. Rev.).

Transliteration, Translation and Commentary

Chapter I

Tablet 13963, Plate 10, Hymn to Bel

Obverse

1. *ù-mu-un na-àm-zu-ka na-àm-* . . . . *še-ir-ma-al nì*(IM)-[*te-na*]
O lord of wisdom, ... supreme by thyself!

2. *dimmer Mu-ul-lil ù-mu-un na-àm-zu-ka* . . . . *še-ir-ma-al nì*(IM)-*te-na*
O Bêl, lord of wisdom, ... supreme by thyself!

3. *a-a dimmer Mu-ul-lil ù-mu-un-e kur-kur-ra*
O father Bêl, lord of the lands!

4. *a-a dimmer Mu-ul-lil ù-mu-un dug*(KA)-*ga zi*(*d*)-*da*
O father Bêl, lord of righteous command!

5. *a-a dimmer Mu-ul-lil siba sag gig*(MI)-*ga*
O father Bêl, shepherd of the black-headed!

6. *a-a dimmer Mu-ul-lil i-de*(NE) *gaba nì*(IM)-*te-na*
O father Bêl, the only all-seeing one!

7. *a-a dimmer Mu-ul-lil ama erim*(ṢAB)-*na di-di*
O father Bêl, the lord that executest judgment on thy enemies!

8. *a-a dimmer Mu-ul-lil ù-nê*(*r*)-*la ma-ma*
O father Bêl, the power of the lands!

9. *ama nà-a gù ne-sig*(PA) *gan-nu ki*
The bull of the pasture, the bull that encompassest the productive land!

10. *dimmer Mu-ul-lil nin ḳar-ra ki damal-ra*
O Bêl, the bountiful lord of the broad land!

11. *ù-mu-un mu-ud-na dú*(KAK) *sag-ma-al ki*
The lord of creation, the creator, the true head of the land!

12. *ù-mu-un zal*(NI)*-laḫ*(UD)*-na ga nunuz-dm*(A.AN) *da-ma-al-la*
The lord whose shining oil is milk for an extensive progeny!

13. *ù-mu-un silim*(DI)*-ma-a-ni eri ir-ir*
The lord whose decrees bind together the city,

14. *dù nà-a-ni à*(ID) *àm-e gal-la*
Whose powerful dwelling-place (is the seat of) a great command,

15. *kur dimmer Babbar* (UD)*-ê*(UD.DU)*-ta kur dimmer Babbar*(UD)*-šu-šù*(KU)
From the land of the rising sun to the land of the setting sun!

16. *kur-ra ù-mu-un nu-um-ti za-e ù-mu-un ab-da-me-en*
O mountain, the lord of life, thou the lord indeed art!

Reverse

17. *dimmer Mu-ul-lil kur-kur-ra ga-šá-an nu-um-ti nin-zu ga-šá-an ab-da*(*-me-en*)
O Bêl of the lands, lord of life, lord of wisdom, lord indeed thou art!

18. *e-lum nì*(IM) *an-na a-kad za-da šá mu-e-da-mal*(IG)
O mighty one, dread of heaven, royal one indeed thou art!

19. *dimmer Mu-ul-lil u en*(?) *dimmer-ri-ne za-da šá mu-e-da-mal*(IG)
O Bêl, very lord of gods thou indeed art!

20. *a-a dimmer Mu-ul-lil mu-lu gu má*(SAR)*-má*(SAR)*-me-en mu-lu še má*(SAR)*-má*(SAR)*-me-en*
O father Bêl, who causest vegetation to sprout, who causest grain to grow

21. *dimmer Mu-ul-lil me-lam*(NE)*-zu gúr*(KIL)*-ra ḫa mu-ni-ib-*( )*-ne-ne*
O Bêl, before thy great glory may they be (in fear?)!

22. *ḫu-e an-na ḫa-e ṭú*(r)*-ra šà*(LIB)*-nì*(IM) *ma-ni-ib-si*
The birds of heaven and the fish of the sea are filled with fear of thee!

23. *a-a dimmer Mu-ul-lil-li da-da maḫ mu-e-gin*(DU) *sag-e-zi si-ba-e e-nab*
O father Bêl, in great strength thou goest, the head of life, the shepherd of the stars!

24. *ù-mu-un ka- na-àm-gá*(MAL) *iz-ba eri ga mu-e-gin*(DU) *gín*(GI) *si ti-šù*(KU) *me-a*
O lord, the mouth of production thou openest, as a prolific city thou goest, the reed for the fulness of life thou art.

25. *a-a* [dimmer] *Mu-ul-lil sag zi sag nê*(r)*-la šú ti ba-ni-ib-ag*
O father Bêl, the head of life, the head of strength, the power of life thou makest thyself!

26. *šú-gil niš-ia mu-bi im*
Altogether there are twenty-five lines in the tablet.

27. *êr*(A.ŠI) *lim-ma*
Hymn of praise.

This composition is a hymn of praise to Bêl, who is directly addressed. His name, Mu-ul-lil, appears in 14 of the 25 lines of the hymn, in which he is called distinctively "father", the title occurring 8 times.

The god is addressed in the second person, as is seen in line 16, where *za-e*, the personal pronoun of the second person, is applied to him, and also in the pronominal phase of the second person, *za-da*, found in lines 18 and 19, not to mention other less striking symbols of the second person singular.

The hymn consists of many laudatory epithets descriptive of Bêl's divine nature and work. His fatherhood and lordship are dwelt upon. He is a righteous and all-wise father. His lordship extends not only over the land, but up into the air as well. He provides subsistence for the creatures of earth, being also the organizer of city and state. He superintends also the operations of nature in the atmosphere being the dread of heaven, the lord of gods, the occasion of fear among the birds and fishes, the shepherd of the storms (or stars).

The time of the origin of this hymn is a matter of conjecture. The form of the signs offers some evidence. What the early kings say of Bêl also throws some light on the subject. The signs are, of course, later than the picture-writing of the hieroglyph, and also later than the linear script suited to stone. These signs are made in clay, hence the wedge appears. The design of the signs used here has met with some transformation since the hieroglyph was used, but it has not yet reached the chaste and symmetrical form given by the hand of the Assyrian. In short the signs of this hymn are old Babylonian, almost identical with those used in the inscriptions of Eannatum, Entemena, Gudea and Ḫammurabi. There are, however, some later and even New-Babylonian signs among them, pointing perhaps to transcription subsequent to the original composition.

There is no mention of any city in the hymn, as there is in the hymn to Sin, but this hymn probably had its origin in Nippur which was the great religious centre of Babylonia in the predynastic period, when kings ascribed their successes to Bêl and brought their booty to Nippur, calling Bêl "the lord of the lands."

Obverse

1. *ù-mu-un na-àm-zu-ka na-àm* . . . . . *še-ir-ma-al nì-[te-na]*
O lord of wisdom, ... supreme by thyself!

ù-mu-un means "being lord", *ù* equalling "lord" and *mu-un* equalling "being". *ù-mu-un* is a phonetic representation of *umun* = *bêlu*, (Br. 9475). *umun* is sometimes ideographically represented by the sign GIGURÛ, the corner wedge (Br. 8659), which signifies "depress", "overpower", "be powerful", "rule". *umun* may be shortened either to *u*, *mun* or *un*, giving to GIGURÛ three values for "lord", *u*, *un* and *umun*. *umun*, which is ES, has an EK value, *ugun*. In line 17, we shall meet with another word for "lord"; viz., *ga-šá-an*.

ù: the sign IGI-DIBBU alone means "lord". It has a well-known Assyrian equivalent, *labâru*, "be old", (Br. 9464). Brummer explains the sign correctly as follows: IGI-DIBBU is a compound sign and equals ŠI, "eye", plus LU, "take away", hence the meaning "take away the eye", "become old", "elderly", "lord", (SVA. 2—7).

mu-un contracted to *mun* is cognate with *me-en* which equals *bašû*, "to be", as in *za-e-me-en* (Br. 10404). We shall meet the form *mu-un* as a verbal prefix.

mu here is simply a dialectic form of *me* (MSL., p. 240). *mu* as a Sumerian value is attested by the sign-name MU. We shall meet with MU in the name *Mu-ul-lil*, also as a suffix and in other ways The MU of our text is old Babylonian. It is the MU of Ur-Gur and Gudea (see brick of Ur-Gur, No. 90009, CT. XXI, and Gudea's Cylinder A, Col. XVIII, line 27, in Déc. 36).

un is plainly cognate with *en* which is so commonly represented by the sign ÊNU. The sign UN we shall meet again with the value *kalama*. The UN of our text is a very ancient sign (see Cone of Eannatum, Col. I, CT. XXI, Tablet 80062).

na-àm-zu-ka consists of noun, *na-àm-zu* and postposition *ka*.

na-àm-zu is an abstract noun composed of the abstract prefix *na-àm* and the stem *zu*.

na-àm equals *šîmtu*, "fortune", (Br. 1609 and HW. 654) and is a dialectic form of *nam* (Br. 2103) which is a common abstract prefix.

na is a Sumerian value of the sign NANÛ. The value is simply syllabic here. The sign originally signified "stone". Our

NA is found both in old Babylonian tablets and in New-Babylonian inscriptions.

àm (ES) also is only syllabic here. The sign has the EK value *ag* and is used ideographically.

zu: the sign representing *zu* has only one value, presenting a rather uncommon circumstance in Sumerian. *zu* means "know", also "be wise", and may equal *nîmeḳu*, "wisdom", (Br. 136), but the author preferred to say *na-àm-zu*, "the fortune of wisdom".

ḳa, sign-name KÂGU, is a postpositive sign of the genitive. The sign KÂGU (discussed below) is often used in this way, but it has several values and is used to express a large number of ideas. *ḳa* as a postposition is a dialectic form of *ge*(KIT).

še-ìr-ma-al is ES for the EK *nìr-gal*, *š* changing to *n* and *m* to *g* (MSL. p. XI). It is translated into Assyrian by the word *etellu*. *še-ìr-ma-al* consists then of two parts; stem *še-ìr* and suffix *ma-al*. Strictly, *še-ìr* is "lord" and *še-ìr-ma-al* is "lordship".

še-ìr: *e* and *ì* appear generally to be distinct sounds, but they combine, just as the two *u*'s combine in *mu-un*, making *mun*, and as the two *a*'s combine in *na-àm*, making *nam*. Evidently the weaker sound is absorbed by the stronger, hence *še-ìr* becomes *šêr*, "ruler", which could be represented by NISIGÛ (JA., 1905, p. 113, also Br. 4306).

še is perhaps a Semitic value coming from *šê'u*, "grain". The original sign is a picture of a head of grain like wheat or oats. The name of the sign is Û-UM. The sign occurs in line 20 as an ideogram.

ìr is also Semitic value of the sign GAḲ-GUNÛ We shall meet the sign used as a verb equal to *kamû*, "bind".

ma-al, phonetically written for *mal*, is an ending which adds to *šêr* the idea of "having"; hence *še-ìr-ma-al* means "having rule".

ma: we shall find MAMÛ used mostly as a noun, but it may occur as a verbal prefix or as a phonetic complement.

al: the sign has only one value, *al*, whose use is principally syllabic. The sign-name is ALLU.

nì-te-na: *nì-te* is the main word with *na* as a suffix.

nì-te: *nì* and *te* stand related to each other as object and cognate verb, meaning "fear a fear". The affinity of *nì* and *te* is shown by the fact that the sign for *nì*, called IMMU, may have the value *tu* (see Br. 8355), then the object and verb would be *tu-te*, "fear a fear" (see Fossey in JA., 1905, p. 128). *nì-te* may mean "self" just as *nì* may stand not only for "fear" but for that which causes fear as *Rammânu*, "the storm-god", and then by way of erroneous association for *ramânu*, "self".

nì: the sign IMMU is one of the principal signs that originally denoted "the quarter of the heavens". It is used to signify „storm" and many ideas connected with storm.

te: TÊMMÊNU originally meant "orientation", then "to approach hostilely"; hence *nì-te* meant "approach of storm".

na is an indeterminate suffix, but the context shows that it means "thy", so that *nì-te-na* means "thyself" (see *na* above).

2. dimmer *Mu-ul-lil ù-mu-un na-àm-zu-ka . . . . še-ir-ma-al nì-te-na*

O Bêl, lord of wisdom, ... supreme by thyself!

dimmer: the sign AN here has the value *dimmer*. In the great bilingual penitential Psalm, K. 2811 (IV R. plate 10), instead of the single sign AN, we have the spelling *dim-me-er* (see lines 3, 7 and others). If this were an EK composition, the sign AN might be *dingir*, *di-in-gir*, but in the words *ù-mu-un* and *še-ir-ma-al* which we have already had, we have evidence that this is an ES composition, hence AN here is to be read *dimmer*.

Mu-ul-lil: Bêl has only one name in this hymn; namely, *Mul-lil*. In the two tablets, 29644 and 29623, following this tablet, Bêl is called *En-lil* (see the colophons). The word *Mu-ul-lil* divides into two parts, *Mu-ul*, which contracts into *Mul*, and *lil*.

Mu-ul: *Mul* is ES; *En* is EK. Both *Mul* and *En* mean "lord", so that either *Mul-lil* or *En-lil* means "lord of fulness". It is probable that *mul* (*wul*) is cognate with *en* (el).

mu (as a value is discussed in line 1).

ul: the sign is composed of GÊŠPU and GUṬṬU. The value *ul* is Semitic. We shall meet below this sign with the value *rù* meaning "perfect".

lil: the name of the sign is KÎTU. *lil* in magic writings means "demon", i. e., a spirit which may be either good or bad. Originally the sign indicated "structure", from which idea comes the postpositional use of the sign with the value *ge*. *šâru*, "wind", with the value *lil* is a secondary meaning of thes sign.

ù-mu-un na-àm-zu-ka (occurring in line 1, was discussed there). The fragments following *-ka* do not give a sure clue as to what the signs were before the erasure. After dimmer *Mu-ul-lil* perhaps the whole of the second line was precisely like the first.

še-ir-ma-al nì-te-na (explained in line 1).

3. *a-a* dimmer *Mu-ul-lil ù-mu-un-e kur-kur-ra*

O father Bêl, lord of the lands!

a-a is probably for *ad-da*, *ad* meaning "protector". Exactly how *a-a* comes to be used in the place of *ad-da* may not be determined with certainty. The explanation may lie in the relation between "water", „seed" and "father". *a-a* also seems to be a softened form of *ad-da*. *a* means "seed" or more primarily "water". The sign is an ideographic picture of dripping water.

dimmer Mu-ul-lil (explained in line 2).

ù-mu-un-e divides into the word *ù-mu-un* and the prolongation vowel *e*, possibly demonstrative in sense (see *e* farther on)

ù-mu-un is not elsewhere in this hymn lengthened to *ù-mu-un-e*, but *ù-mu-un* occurs nine times.

kur-kur-ra is the plural form of noun, *kur*, plus postposition *ra*.

kur-kur: in Sumerian the general way of denoting the plural in nouns is by doubling the root (see ASK. p. 140), whereas the doubled root in a verb means an intensified or causative stem. There are five other cases of doubling the root in the hymn: *di-di*, line 7, *ma-ma*, line 8, *ir-ir*, line 13, *má-má*, line 20; and *da-da*, line 23.

kur: the sign KÛRU in the old linear form represented pictorially "mountain tops". The value *kur* has three very common Assyrian equivalents, *šadû*, "mountain", *irṣitu*, "earth" and *mâtu*, "land", all closely related to each other.

ra is a common postposition signifying "unto" Perhaps *ra* sometimes serves merely as a vowel of prolongation, the *r* at the same time making a double of the final consonant of the preceding word. In such a case *ra* is called a phonetic complement, while it also helps to determine the value of the sign immediately preceding. To illustrate, the sign KÛRU being followed by RARÛ cannot be read *gin* nor *mad*. *ra* can also be the sign of the genitive (Br. 6367).

4. *a-a dimmer Mu-ul-lil ù-mu-un dug-ga zi-da*
O father Bêl, lord of righteous command!

a-a dimmer Mu-ul-lil ù-mu-un (explained in lines 1, 2 and 3).

dug-ga: *dug* is the value of KÂGU to be used here, as is at once suggested by the phonetic complement *ga*.

dug: a very common meaning of *dug* is *ḳibîtu*, "command" (Br. 532).

ga is merely the vowel of prolongation *a* with the final *g* of the preceding stem.

zi-da: *zi* being followed by *da* gives the impression that it should be read *zid* with *da* as a phonetic complement. A final consonant in the first syllable, however, is not always a necessity. The name of the temple of Nabu at Borsippa is not read *È-zid-da*, but *È-zi-da* or *È-zida*.

zi here equals *imnu*, "right". It may sometimes equal *napištu* (see below, line 25.)

5. *a-a dimmer Mu-ul-lil siba sag gig-ga*
O father Bêl, shepherd of the blackheaded!

siba equals *rê'û* (Br. 5688). The sign is compounded from PA and LU and means "staff-bearer", since PA signifies "staff" and LU means "hold", "seize". The use of the sign is confined almost entirely to the idea of shepherd of animals and then figuratively to that of governor of men.

sag: the sign with the value *sag*, called SANGU or SAGGU, is the common sign to represent "head" which is expressed in Assyrian either by *rêšu* or *ḳaḳḳadu* (see Br. 3522 and 3513). The sign occurs in many compounds.

gig-ga: *gig* is the value of MI suggested by the phonetic complement *ga*.

gig: the sign is composed of the corner wedge U and the sign TATTAB and means "darkness". The sign really signifies "entering into depression". *gi* perhaps is a dialectism for *mi*.

ga = phonetic complement. *sag gig-ga* means a race of men, evidently here the Babylonians, the people in particular over whom Bêl exercised rule. The term is certainly not one of depreciation. It merely shows that the Babylonians were swarthy. On the other hand, "blackheaded" may be intended to mean the human race inhabiting the earth in contradistinction to the bright celestial beings (see CDAL. 878). Cyrus, in his Broken Cylinder, seems to use the phrase as meaning the Babylonians. His words are: *nišê ṣalmat ḳaḳḳadi šá ú-šá-ak-ši-du ḳa-ta-a-šu.* "The blackheaded people whom he caused his hands to conquer" (V R. 35, 13)

6. *a-a* *dimmer* *Mu-ul-lil i-de gaba nì te-na*
O father Bêl, the only all-seeing one!

i-de, phonetic representation of *ide*, which in the EK dialect is represented by the sign IGÛ with the value *igi* which in Assyrian means *înu*, "eye" (Br. 4004, 4003 and 9273) *ide* is ES for the EK *igi*. We have the sign IGÛ in the colophon where it occurs with ÂU, "water", *a-ide* meaning "water of the eye".

i is represented by GIṬṬÛ ("five"). The value *i*, however, is, of course, entirely syllabic here. Notice that there is a slight difference between the Babylonian GIṬṬÛ and the Assyrian GIṬṬÛ. In Assyrian, GIṬṬÛ consists of two wedges followed by three. In Babylonian it consists of three followed by two, and in the linear form the sign consists of three horizontal lines followed by two (see AL. p. 125, No. 105).

de represented by IZÛ and having the value *bil* means "fire". The sign in its hieroglyphic form is probably a picture of building a fire by the friction of an instrument against a piece of wood. Hence the sign is properly composed of AM and GIŠ, AM representing something having a head and GIŠ meaning "wood". The sign in our text is old Babylonian and may be found in Gudea

(Cylinder B, Col. IV, line 13, in Déc. Plate 34). Possibly *i-de* could be explained as if *i* were an abstract prefix and *de* as referring to the light of the eye, hence *i-de* means "eye".

gaba is the common word for *irtu*, "breast" (Br. 4477). The sign GABBU is a double MU-sign meaning "fulness". From this idea of "fulness" we easily derive the idea of "open" (Br. 4490). So that *ide gaba* means "open eyed" The two MU's appear entirely separate in the Babylonian form of the sign as they do not in the Assyrian form (see TC. p. 18). Our GABBU is not so old as the GABBU of the *Stèle des Vautours*, but is like Gudea's GABBU (see Cylinder A, Col. XXI, line 25, in Déc. Plate 34). *i-de gaba* is about equal to "omniscient".

nì-te-na may be rendered as in line 1, "thyself," or perhaps we could say "only".

7. *a-a* *dimmer* *Mu-ul-lil ama erim-na di-di*

O father Bêl, the lord that executest judgment on thy enemies!

ama: the meaning for AMMU with the value *ama* is *rîmu*, "bull". AMMU may mean "lord", *bêlu* (Br. 4543). In the sign AMMU we have the hieroglyphs for the bull's head and the mountain combined. In the oldest Babylonian form, of course, lines are used instead of wedges. In Assyrian the sign has been reduced to two horizontal wedges placed before the sign DÛGU AMMU represents "the bull of the mountains". In line 9 we shall have the sign GUṬṬU which represents "the bull not of the mountains", i e. "the domestic bull" or "the ox". The sign is the same in form as AMMU, except that the little inside wedges representing the mountains are wanting.

erim-na: *erim* is taken to be the right value rather than *laḫ*, because of the following *na* which serves as a phonetic complement, *m* and *n* being closely related because of their similar indeterminate nasal qualities.

erim affords a meaning that seems to suit the context. *erim* must be equal to the Assyrian *ṣâbu* which must like the Hebrew *ṣābā* have in it the idea of "service". Such expressions as the following bring out the idea of "service". *erim-bal-ku-a*, "slave employed at the water wheel" (OBTR. Plate 91, Obv). *erim-bal-gub-ba*, "slave who carries a hatchet" (OBTR. Plate 17, Obv.). A common meaning for *erim* is "warrior", but the warrior as a soldier rather a general. Then from the idea "soldier of the enemy", we come to the idea "enemy", which seems to be the meaning here.

na, while serving phonetically, is also here a pronominal suffix.

di-di can equal *kašâdu* (Br. 9529 and 9563). The judgment implied by *di-di*, accordingly, may be that executed on an enemy.

di-di is more than pronouncing sentence. It is inflicting the punishment.

di may be a value borrowed from the Assyrian *dânu*, "to judge", but this is uncertain, as such an occurrence implies Semitic influence which could not have amounted to much if this hymn was written at a very early period.

8. *a-a dimmer Mu-ul-lil ù-nê-la ma-ma*
O father Bêl, the power of the land!

ù-nê-la equals noun *ù-nê* = *emûḳu*, "power" and phonetic complement *la*.

ù: IGI-DIBBU might be confounded with ḪUL. It is rather carelessly written here. *ù*, we have seen in line 1, may mean "lord" in the sense of being "elderly". *ù* might mean "mountain"; if so it would be in the sense of being an "ancient mountain". *ù* here, however, must be an abstract prefix (MSL. p. XVII). *ù*, for example, is used as such a prefix with *tu*, *ù-tu* being equal to "offspring" (Br. 9470).

nê: PIRIḲḲU in passing from the old Babylonian form which we have in our text meets with much change. The form in our text comes near to being that of the oldest known. Even in Ḫammurabi it begins to take the form of the Assyrian PIRIḲḲU (see CḤ. XLIV. 24. Plate LXXXI). PIRIḲḲU with the value *gir* which is EK for the ES *ner* is the common sign for "foot" (Br. 9192). With the meaning of "power" it generally has the value *nê* (Br. 9184).

la: LALÛ here is essentially the same as the old linear picture which may readily be found in old Sumerian script, given also by Delitzsch (see AL. p. 122, No. 31). *la* means "fulness" like the Assyrian *lalû*, but its use in our text is entirely phonetic. We should rather expect *ra* here. Note that in line 10, we have *ra* where we should expect *la*, and in line 12, we have *da-ma-al-la* where the *la* is regular, just as *ra* is regular in *kur-kur-ra* of line 3.

ma-ma: MAMÛ in its original form is an old hieroglyph representing the earth, so that "earth" or "the land" is a common meaning for *ma* and equal to the Assyrian *mâtu* which probably comes from Sumerian *ma*, "land", and *da*, "strong" = DADDU (see line 1 for further comment).

9. *ama nà-a gù ne-sig gan-nu ki*
The bull of the pasture, the bull that encompassest the productive land.

ama, which in line 7 was rendered by "lord", must mean here "bull", as the word *nà-a* limits us to this meaning. *nà-a* means "pasture". *nà-a* could be taken as an adjective, descriptive of the attitude of the bull, i. e., that of lying down quietly. We have *nà-a* again in line 14. *a* is simply phonetic here (see line 3)

nà: the sign for the value *nà* has no sign-name. In almost this form, the sign is easily found in the text of Gudea (see Cylinder B, Col. XVI, line 19, in Déc. 35). The form in our text is very near to the original linear form and differs much from the Assyrian. The ordinary meaning of *nà* is given by the Assyrian *rabâṣu* "lie down", kindred to the Hebrew *rābăṣ*.

gù, the value here for GUṬṬU, is commonly rendered in Assyrian by *alpu* "ox". The sign represents the bull's head with horns. Historically the sign has three forms, the old Babylonian linear form, the old Babylonian wedge-form and the Assyrian wedge-form. The old Babylonian linear and wedge-forms are the same, except that wedges occur in the latter where simple straight lines appear in the former. The Assyrian form is composed of two horizontal wedges, one upright wedge and two little corner wedges (AL. p 128, No. 164). The difference between GUṬṬU aad AMMU is significant (see note on line 7).

ne-sig: *ne-sig-ga* equals *kamû*, "bind" (Br. 4626). The meaning "bind" fits here.

ne is not an unusual indeterminate verbal prefix (see MSL. p. XXIX).

sig = PA, probably with the value *sig*, may equal *kamû* (Br. 5575). Hence *ne-sig* is a verb, *ne* being the prefix and *sig* the stem.

gan-nu: the value *gan* is indicated by the following *nu*.

gan with complementary *nu* is represented here by an ancient form of the sign which is very different from the Assyrian form. The meaning here must be expressed by *daḫâdu*, "plenty", kindred to *alidu* (IV R. 9, 24 a).

ki: the KIKÛ of our text is New-Babylonian (see the Cyrus Cylinder, I R. 35, line 4). The early linear form is well represented by the wedge-form of Ḫammurabi (CḪ. Col. I, line 10, plate I). A picture of the earth was probably attempted in the archaic linear form. It should be noted that space is represented conventionally by parallel horizontal lines included in a rectangle, orientated to the four quarters of the heavens.

10. *dimmer Mu-ul-lil nin ḳar-ra ki damal-ra*
O Bêl, the bountiful lord of the broad land!

dimmer Mu-ul-lil (see line 2 for notes).

nin in the sense of *bêlu*, "lord", gives a good context.

ḳar-ra equals noun *ḳar* and postposition *ra*; *ḳar* = "plenty" (see MSL. 123). The text however may be *dam-ḳar-ra*.

Note that *ra* may be taken as a postposition of the genitive as well as phonetic complement (see on line 3).

ki (see on line 9).

damal-ra equals adjective plus postposition.

damal, ES for the EK *dagal*, with the meaning of *rapšu*, "extensive" (Br. 5452). The sign name is AMÛ. The sign is composed of two signs one within the other, PISANNU, "house", the outer sign, and ANÛ, "high", the inner sign, hence the meaning "large space", "extensive".

11. *ù-mu-un mu-ud-na dú sag-ma-al ki*
The lord of creation, the creator, the true head of the land!

ù-mu-un (see line 1 for note).

mu-ud-na may equal "creator" or "begetter", just as *muḫ-na* equals the Assyrian *a-lid* (IV R 9, 32 a). *mu-ud* is a phonetic representation of the word *mud*, whose sign is MUŠÊN-DUGÛ, ḪU plus ḪI (Br. 2273). The word *mud* is equal to the Assyrian *banû* (Br. 2274).

dú: here we must let the sense govern us in deciding on a form which may be read either as KAK or NI. KAK with the value *du* equal to *banû* (Br. 5248) gives a meaning that fits smoothly with what precedes and follows. In their original forms KAK, NI and IR are similar yet entirely distinct signs. In the archaic linear form, KAK is a triangle with one of the angles pointing to the right. NI is a triangle with one of the angles pointing to the right and one upright line passing through the triangle. IR also is a triangle with one of the angles pointing to the right and two upright lines passing through the triangle.

sag-ma-al equals noun *sag*, plus suffix *ma-al*. It could stand for *sag-ga* just as *sag-mal* can stand for *sag-ga* (Br. 3595). *sag* equals "head" (as in line 5). *ma-al*: if *ma-al* is taken a suffix (as in line 1), it stands for the sign PISANNU meaning *šakânu*, "establish", or *bašû*, "exist", and is ES for the EK *gal*.

ki (see line 9).

12. *ù-mu-un zal laḫ-na ga nunuz-ám da-ma-al-la*
The lord whose shining oil is milk for an extensive progeny!

ù-mu-un (see line 1 for note).

zal: NI means "oil". The Babylonian KAK, NI and IR should be distinguished from the Assyrian. In Assyrian the horizontal wedges are parallel and do not come to an angle at the right.

laḫ-na: *zal laḫ-na* means "his shining oil", and the thought appears to be that Bêl causes food to be produced to sustain successive generations. His oil is milk for many generations.

zal-laḫ is somewhat like the expression "finest oil" found in Assyrian inscriptions.

laḫ: the signs ḪISSU and ṢÂBU find their nearest approach to each other in the value *laḫ*. Both signs have this value with the meaning "brightness".

na here is a suffix of the third person; sometimes it is second person (see line 1).

ga: our sign here is the old Babylonian GÛ which with its common value *ga* means *šizbu*, "milk". The archaic linear form represents the teat of the breast. *ga* occurs often as a phonetic complement (see line 4).

nunuz-ám means "is multitudinous". *nunuz*: NUNUZ in this form is, as Delitzsch observes (HW. p 525b), New-Babylonian. In Assyrian it is composed of ṢAB and ḪI and in New-Babylonian of ṢAB and ŠE. Here it is equal to the Assyrian *lîpu*, German "Nachkomme".

ám: A.AN, equalling *ám*, is a well recognized verbal suffix used like the verb "to be"; for instance, *dingir-ra ám* means "is a god" and *gal-la ám* means "is great" (see SVA. p. 56)

da-ma-al-la is composed of the adjective *da-ma-al* and the phonetic complement *la*. *da-ma-al* is the phonetic representation in ES of the sign AMÛ meaning *rapšu* (see line 10).

13. *ù-mu-un silim-ma-a-ni eri ir-ir*
The lord whose decrees bind together the city.

silim-ma-a-ni means "his decree". Thus, *silim-ma-a* equals noun, plus phonetic complement, plus vowel prolongation. *silim*· we have had the sign SARARÛ (in line 7), where it was given the value *di*; here, however, the phonetic complement suggests the choice of the value *silim*, from which we derive the meaning "decree", although "salutation" is a more primary meaning expressed by the Semitic value *silim* (from *šulmu*). The sign is apparently New-Babylonian.

ni is one of the common nominal suffixes of the third person. Note that Bêl is addressed in the third person in this line, but we shall find him addressed in the second person again in line 16.

eri is ES for the EK *uru*. This value is substantiated by the name of the city of Eridu = *Eri-ṭu* (see MSL p. 105). The name of the sign is ALU. Our sign is old Babylonian and is not very different from the hieroglyphic form which is supposed to represent a city (see AL. p 121, No. 21). It differs considerably from the New-Babylonian ALU which is much like the Assyrian.

ir-ir is an intensive form of the verb and therefore may be causative. Bêl is supposed to have aided kings especially in capturing cities. *ir* may mean "bind", expressed by *kamû*, but *kamû* is not so often represented by IR as by DIBBU or LALLU. *kamû* may be represented by PA (see line 9). Although *ìr* is said to be a Semitic value, it is used in this hymn syllabically and is the only value of the sign preserved (see line 1 and also *dù* in line 11 for further comment).

14. *dù nà-a-ni à àm-e gal-la*
Whose powerful dwelling-place (is the seat of) a great command,

dù: the sign giving this value has two origins, one of which is represented by the value *dul*, meaning "cover" (Br. 9582). The other is represented by the value *dù* and means "dwelling-place", rendered in Assyrian by *šubtu* (Br. 9588). *dù* really means "prescribed space".

nà-a-ni means "his lying-down place". *nà-a* defines with more particularity the nature of the dwelling as "a lying-down place", "a permanent place of rest". Here we have *dù nà-a*; above we have *ama nà-a* (line 9).

à: IDU and DADDU come from the same ideogram which is the picture of the hand and the forearm, the fingers pointing to the left. The value *id* is supposed to be of Semitic derivation, from the root appearing in Assyrian as *idu*, "hand". The sign IDU also means "side", "wing", "horn", "power". Hence I render "powerful" here, making it qualify *dù nà-a-ni*. The sign in our text is old Babylonian; yet it seems to be a form that is approaching the Assyrian form. TA is also related to ID and DA and is used as DA sometimes is, as a postposition.

àm-e, composed of prefix *àm* and stem *e*. *àm*: we have had the sign used phonetically (line 1). Here it is undoubtedly an abstract prefix (MSL. p. XVII), qualifying the following *e*. The sign is old Babylonian, readily found in old Babylonian inscriptions. It is a composite sign. The enclosure contains the sign IZÛ which is also composite. IZÛ however, as explained above (line 6), means "fire". So *àm* is primarily the "fire of love", hence the usual meaning "love".

e: it is clear that *e* can equal *ḳabû*, "speak" (Br. 5843 and HW. 578a). Hence *àm-e* must mean "speech". The sign is old Babylonian, as may be seen, for instance, by examining Hammurabi. It is called ÊGÛ. The New-Babylonian form comes nearer to the old Babylonian than the Assyrian does. This fact goes to show that the Assyrian signs are as a rule farther away from the archaic forms than the New-Babylonian signs are. The sign ÂU represented "water", but the sign ÊGÛ represented the "waterditch", "canal". How *e* comes to mean *ḳabû* may perhaps be explained by its relation to the value *i* of KÂGU which equals *amâtu*, "word".

gal-la: *gal*, "great", is often followed by the phonetic complement *la*.

15. *kur* *dimmer* *Babbar-ê-ta kur* *dimmer* *Babbar-šu-šù*
From the land of the rising sun to the land of the setting sun!

kur (see on line 3).

dimmer *Babbar-ê-ta* equals ideogram for "the sun", plus verb *ê* = "coming out", plus postposition "from". *dimmer* *Babbar* is the ordinary ideogram for *ilu* *Šamaš* used of "the sun", as well as of "the god *Šamaš*". *Babbar* is a value of HISSU which means "to be white".

ê: = two signs, UD and DU, equivalent to this value, meaning *aṣû*, "come out", or "go out". The sign UD is a picture of the sun, and represents the rising sun; hence = "come forth".

ta is a postposition meaning in this case "from", but often "in, into". TA in our text is old Babylonian and much like the linear form in early tablets. Nearly the same form can be found in Ḥammurabi also. But on the whole, the old Babylonian, the Assyrian and the New-Babylonian all differ from each other much. TA has a close relation to DA and ID (see on line 14).

dimmer *Babbar-šu-šù* equals ideogram for "the sun", plus *šu* = "going in", plus postposition "to".

šu equals *erêbu*, "enter in". Ideographically, ŠU means "bent over", or "depressed".

šù is a value of KU, as a postposition, meaning "unto". The sign is of rectangular form and has many values, consequently many meanings starting with the idea "enclosure". The governing force of *šù* here reaches back over *kur* in the middle of the line, just as the governing force of *ta* goes back over *kur* at the beginning of the line.

The beautiful expression of this line occurs more than once in Sumerian and Babylonian literature. As early as Lugalziggisi it appears in royal writings. Lugalziggisi speaks of his kingdom as extending "from the rising sun to the setting sun". *Babbar-ê-ta* (UD.UD DU.TA) *Babbar-šu-šù* (UD.ŠU.KU) (OBI. No. 87, Col. II, 12 and 13). And Esarhaddon in Cylinder A says that "From the rising sun to the setting sun he marched without a rival". *ul-tu ṣi-it* *ilu* *Šam-ši a-di e-rib* *ilu* *Šam-ši it-tal-lak-u-ma ma-ḫi-ra la i-šu-u* (I R. 45, Col. I, 7 and 8).

16. *kur-ra ù-mu-un nu-um-ti za-e ù-mu-un ab-da-me-en*
O mountain, the lord of life, thou the lord indeed art!

kur-ra (see on line 3).

ù-mu-un (see on line 1).

nu-um-ti occurs also in the next line and no doubt equals *balâṭu*, "life".

nu-um seems to be an abstracting prefix of the nature of *nam* as in *nam-ti-la* = *balâṭu* (Br. 1697). *nu-um-ti*, however, may be a phonetic representation of *nim*, also written *num* which means *elîtu*, "height" (Br. 1982 and 9011). According to this view, *nu-um-ti* might mean "the acme of life", just as *nam-ti* equals "the fortune of life"; hence "life in general". Or it might be suggested that *num* is really for *nam*, as *a* is known to differentiate sometimes into *u*; *ga* for instance becomes *gu* (MSL. p. X).

ti equals *balâṭu*, "life", and has its fuller form in *tin*, also equal to *balâṭu* "live".

za-e equals *atta*, "thou" (Br. 11762, also ASK. p 139).

ab-da-me-en equals "thou thyself art". The form consists of verbal prefix, infix and verb, as follows: *ab*, being an indeterminate prefix, may therefore be used of the second person (MSL. p. XXV). ÈŠU is an old Babylonian sign pictorially representing "enclosed space", hence the meaning of "enclosure". It means, with the value *éš*, "house", and, with the value *ab*, "sea". *da* is like *à*(ID) (line 14), ideographically represented by the picture of the hand and forearm (line 4). It means "side", also "strength". It is sometimes a reflexive verbal infix (MSL p. XXIV). *me-en* equals *bašû* (Br. 10404). *me* also equals *bašû* (Br. 10361) and the longer *me-a* equals *bašû* (Br. 10459). *en*, therefore, is not an essential part of the word which means "be". *me-en* has no connection with *ma-e*, the personal pronoun of the first person. *men*, in fact, can be used of the second person and even of the third as well. The defining pronoun *za-e* here compels us to take *me-en* in the second person.

Reverse

17. *dimmer Mu-ul-lil kur-kur-ra ga-šá-an nu-um-ti nin-zu ga-šá-an ab-da(-me-en)*

O Bêl of the lands, lord of life, lord of wisdom, lord indeed thou art!

dimmer Mu-ul-lil (see line 2 for note).

kur-kur-ra (see line 3 for note).

ga-šá-an, like *ù-mu-un* (line 1), equals *bêlu*, "lord", and is a phonetic form of *gašan* which is usually represented by GÊŠPU-GUNÛ (Br 6989 and MSL. p. 129). *ga* is only a syllable here (see lines 4 and 12 for further comment). ŠÁ is an old sign; here it is old Babylonian and represents closely the linear form. The sign is much used in Assyrian with the syllabic value *šá*, especially in the place of NITÛ(ša) which is often a relative pronoun.

nu-um-ti (see on line 16).

nin-zu means "lord of wisdom". *nin* equals *bêlu* (Br. 10985; see line 10). On *zu* (see line 1).

ab-da should evidently be *ab-da-me-en* (see line 16).

18. *e-lum nì an-na a-kad za-da šá mu-e-da-mal*
O mighty one, dread of heaven, royal one indeed thou art!

e-lum equals *kabtu* (Br. 5888), and appears to stand for *elim* which also equals *kabtu* (Br. 8885). *lum* is clearly syllabic here, but the sign, old Babylonian here, is indicative of plant-growth, consisting of waving lines.

nì equals *puluḫtu*, "fear", here (see on line 1).

an-na: *an* equaling *šamê*, "heavens", is a value of ANÛ attested by the phonetic complement *na*. The sign ANÛ in our text is old Babylonian and is the same as the original ideogram of the star, except that wedges have taken the place of straight lines. In our Hymn to Adad (CT. XV, Tablet 29631) the transition from the Babylonian to the Assyrian ANÛ may be clearly seen all on one page, wedges however are used, not straight lines. There is the original form, there is the Assyrian form, and there are intermediate forms enough to show how the Babylonian star passes into the Assyrian ANÛ. The NANÛ of our text may be found exactly in the Brick of Ur-Gur (CT. XXI, Tablet 90000, plate 8). In Nebuchadrezzar I. (CT. IX, Tablet 92987), the internal horizontals have disappeared, but the sign has not fully reached the Assyrian NANÛ.

a-kad: perhaps this word *a-kad* is a loan-word from the Assyrian *ekdu*. It is better to take *a* as a vocalic abstract prefix and to consider *kad* as the root. There are three signs that give this value *kad* (Br. 1364, 1365 and 2700). The sign GADU means *kitû*, "clothing material" (Br. 2704 and WH. 361; see also MSL. p. 114). The context alone suggests here that some idea of power may be expected in the word *a-kad*. Perhaps royal power is meant, which could be symbolically represented by a garment, especially a royal robe.

za-da no doubt stands for *za-e-da* and would be equal to "thou thyself", "thou indeed" (see line 16).

šá in Sumerian may represent the Assyrian *lû*, "verily", (Br. 7047) *šá*, simply as a syllable, occurs above (see line 17).

mu-e-da-mal is a verb. *mu* is an indeterminate verbal prefix. Whether it is first, second or third person may be determined by the context. Here, however, the *za-da* of the context shows *mu* to be second person (see on line 1). *e* here is a verbal infix, corroborative in character (see MSL. p. XXIV, also lines 3 and 14). *da* is also a verbal infix (see line 16). *mal* equals *bašû*, "to be", (Br. 2238).

19. dimmer *Mu-ul-lil u en*(?) *dimmer-ri-ne za-da šá mu-e-da-mal*
O Bêl, very lord of gods thou indeed art!

u equals *bêlu*, "lord", and is a very common ideogram for "lord" (see *ù-mu-un*, line 1). *en* also equals *bêlu*, "lord", but evidently the text is imperfect at this point (see line 16, on *en*).

dimmer-ri-ne means "gods". *ri* is a phonetic complement; *ne* is a purely phonetic plural ending used both for nouns and verbs (see SVA. p. 69).

za-da šá mu-e-da-mal (see line 18).

20. *a-a* dimmer *Mu-ul-lil mu-lu gu má-má-me-en mu-lu še má-má-me-en*
O father Bêl, who causest vegetation to sprout, who causest grain to grow!

a-a dimmer *Mu-ul-lil* (see on lines 2 and 3).

mu-lu is a phonetic representation of *mulu* (Br. 6398). *mulu* is ES; EK would be *gulu* (Br. 6395). *mu-lu* frequently means the Assyrian relative pronoun *ša* (Br. 6406).

gu: GÛ is a composite sign whose original parts are NI and BE and which means "full of death". According to the derivation, GÛ then may be read as "destruction" (MSL. p. 156). GÛ has also an Assyrian equivalent *gû* meaning "plant", "vegetation" (Br. 11138 and HW. p 582). The consideration of GÛ as meaning "vegetation" looks only on the perishable side of the object. The sign has few values. Here, it is clearly old Babylonian resembling the linear form.

má-má-me-en here equals *aṣû*, "go out", used of plants and trees Br. 4303). The more generally used word for *aṣû* is *ê* (UD.DU) (see on line 15).

má: the name of the sign is NISIGÛ (see note on *še-ir*, line 1). The sign is old Babylonian here. *me-en* (see on line 16).

še: the sign is old Babylonian here Its most common Assyrian equivalent is *šê'u*, "grain" (see line 1). If we gave Û-UM the broader meaning of "production", at the same time reading GÛ as "destruction", we would have the fine antithetical parallelism: "O father Bêl, who bringest forth destruction and who bringest forth production." Such a reading would give quite correctly the course of thought, for Bêl is god of the atmosphere, lord of the clouds, and commander of the rain-storms which are either sources of growth on earth or of ruin. On the other hand, the translation which I have adopted seems perhaps preferable.

21. dimmer *Mu-ul-lil me-lam-zu gúr-ra ḫa-mu-ni-ib-*( )*-ne-ne*
O Bêl, before the great glory may they be (in fear?)!

me-lam-zu: from the combination of ME and LAM we get the Assyrian *melammu*, "glory". *me*: MIMÛ with the value *išib* means *ellu*, "bright" (see line 16 for further comment). *lam*: one of the values of IZÛ, seems to equal *išâtu*, "flame", but the usual value of IZÛ for *išâtu* is *bil* (see line 6, *de*), *me-lam* literally means "bright flame". *zu*, besides being an ideogram for *idû*, "know", is the usual pronominal suffix of the second person singular (see on *zu*, line 1), as in this passage.

gúr-ra gives a good sense, though the signs resemble KU and RA giving *šù-ra*, a double postposition. The text however is defective. *gúr-ra* equals *kabtu* (Br. 10183), making the phrase read "before thy great glory". *gúr*: KIL also has the value *gurun* equal to *ebnu*, "fruit" (Br. 10179). *ra* (see on line 3).

ḫa. KÛA is the usual Sumerian sign used with a verb, to give a precative sense as here. The sign here is old Babylonian and resembles the pictorial form which is clearly that of "a fish" (see on line 22). The original pictorial figure is one of the few to be found in which curved lines predominate.

mu-ni-ib-()-ne-ne: strangely enough the verb seems to be omitted in the sentence of this line. Perhaps the omission is due to scribal error. *mu* is a verbal prefix of the third person here (see on line 18). *ni-ib* is a verbal infix (see MSL. p. XXXIII). The infixes are generally personally indeterminate. They incorporate, between the verbal prefixes that represent the subject and the verb, the object in pronominal form, whether it be direct or indirect. *ni-ib* really equals "before it". The translation disregards *ni-ib* for the sake of smoothness. *ni* (see on line 13). *ib* stands to *ni* as postposition to pronoun. The sign for *ib* is old Babylonian; it is really composite and signifies "side". *ne-ne* is a personal pronoun of the third person (see ASK. p. 139). *ne* is syllabic here (see *de*, line 6, about its ideographic value; also *lam*, line 21).

22. *ḫu-e an-na ḫa-e ṭú-ra šà-nì ma-ni-ib-si*
The birds of the heavens and the fish of the sea are filled with fear of thee!

ḫu-e equals *iṣṣuru*, "bird". *ḫu*. simple *ḫu* is used elsewhere for *iṣṣûru*. The sign MUŠÊNNU here is old Babylonian. The archaic form is supposed to be the picture of a bird in flight. *mušên*, another value of MUŠÊNNU, also means "bird". *e* is not a necessary part of the word, being here only a vowel of prolongation probably indicating the definite article (see lines 3 and 14).

an-na (see on line 18).

ḫa-e equals *nûnu*, "fish". *ḫa* alone equals *nûnu* (see on line 21). *e* serves the same purpose as in *ḫu-e*.

ṭú-ra equals *apsû*, "sea". *ṭú* alone equals *apsû* (Br. 10217). *ra* may be taken as a sign of the genitive (see on line 3).

šà-nì equals "in the midst of fear". *šà*: ŠÂGU, with the

value *šà*, equal to *libbu* or *kirbu*, is one of the few Sumerian prepositions. It precedes its object as a noun in the construct state. *nì* (see on line 18).

ma-ni-ib-si consists of prefix, infix and verb. *ma* is not a very common verbal prefix. It is indeterminate, but the sense requires the third person (see MSL. p. XXIV). *ni-ib* is second person here (see on line 21). *si*: the most common meaning of *si* is *malû*, "fill". The sign is Babylonian and can be found either in the Code of Ḥammurabi or the Cyrus Cylinder.

23. *a-a* *dimmer* *Mu-ul-lil-li da-da maḫ mu-e-gin sag-e-zi si-ba-e e-nab*

O father Bêl, in great strength thou goest, the head of life, the shepherd of the stars!

a-a *dimmer* *Mu-ul-lil-li* (see on line 2). *li* is merely phonetic complement. We might give it an ideographic value and connect it with *da-da* and render "abundant in strength". The common meaning of LILÛ is *rašû*, "abound". With the value *gub*, however, it means *ellu*, "bright". The sign is old Babylonian, yet quite different from the archaic linear form.

da-da means "strength" (see on line 16).

maḫ has three common Assyrian equivalents, *ma'adu*, "many", *rabû*, "great" and *ṣîru*, "high". *maḫ* here equals *rabû*. There is still another Assyrian equivalent, *maḫḫu* which must be a loan-word in Semitic.

mu-e-gin as prefix, infix and verb means "he indeed goes". *mu-e* (see on line 18). *gin* is a value of the sign ARAGUBBÛ (see *ê*, line 15).

sag-e-zi equals "head" (line 5) plus vowel of prolongation (line 3) and "of life" (line 4). ZÎTU equals *napištu* as well as *imnu* and *kînu*.

si-ba-e divides into *siba* and *e*. *si-ba* is the same as *siba* (line 5), only here the word is given syllabically rather than ideographically. *e* is a vowel prolongation (as in line 3).

e-nab is naturally treated as though *e* were a vocalic prefix and *nab* the root. *e* as an abstract prefix, no doubt, is possible (MSL. p. XVII). *nab*: instead of NABBU, perhaps the sign is ANA-ÊŠŠÊKU with the last component omitted; then the value should be *mul*, equal to *kakkabâni*, "stars", and the clause reads: "shepherd of the stars". *e* may equal *mû* "water" (see line 14), and *nab* may equal *šamû*, "heaven"; then we have the reading: "shepherd of the water of heaven".

24. *ù-mu-un ka na-àm-gá iz-ba eri ga mu-e-gin gín si-ti šù-me-a*

O lord, the mouth of production thou openest, as a prolific city thou goest, the reed of the fulness of life thou art!

ù-mu-un (line 1).

ka: KÂGU here is a noun with the value *ka* equal to *pû*, "mouth", (Br. 538). The sign originally represented the head, and its first meaning was *gu* equal to *ḳibû*. The sign is old Babylonian (see on lines 1 and 4).

na-àm-gá is a noun. *na-àm* is an abstract prefix (line 1). *gá* equals *šakânu*, "cause to be", (Br. 5421). The sign is PISANNU. We have had the sign phonetically represented by *ma-al* (line 11) used as a suffix. Here *gá* is not a suffix, but the root.

iz-ba is a verb. *iz* is an indeterminate prefix, shown by the context to be of the second person. *ba* equals *pitû*, "open". The sign is old Babylonian. The archaic form of the sign signified "divide".

eri (see on line 13).

ga (see line 12). *ga* can be used as an adjective meaning "prolific", one of the derived ideas of *ga* as "milk".

mu-e-gin (see line 23).

gín equals *ḳanû*, "reed". The sign is sometimes followed by the phonetic complement *na*. The sign is old Babylonian.

si equals "fulness" (see on line 22).

ti-šù means "unto life". *ti* (see line 16); the sign here, however, really resembles BALA which primarily means "breaking into" Then we have the derived meaning *palû*, "weapon", then "insignia of royal authority", and consequently "rule", "government". If we read *bal* instead of *ti*, then Bêl is "a full reed unto royalty", which makes little sense. *šù* (see line 15).

me-a is the same as *me-en* (see on line 16). *a* is phonetic (see on line 9).

25. *a-a* *dimmer* *Mu-ul-lil sag zi sag nê-la šú ti ba-ni-ib-ag*
O father Bêl, the head of life, the head of strength, the power of life thou makest thyself!

a-a *dimmer* *Mu-ul-lil* (see lines 2 and 3). *sag* (see line 5).

zi equals *napištu* like *ti* (see line 16, also 23). *nê-la* (see on line 8).

šú equals *ḳâtu*, "hand". The sign also has a value *kád* which is evidently derived from the Semitic *ḳâtu*.

ti (see on line 24). If we read the sign as TIL, then Bêl is "the power of life". If we read BALA, then Bêl is "the power of royalty", signifying perhaps that royal authority is vested in Bêl.

ba-ni-ib-ag is a verb. *ba* is an indeterminate verbal prefix, but is much used for the second person (MSL. p. XXVI). *ni-ib* (see on line 21). *ag* equals *epêšu*, "make". The sign is old Babylonian.

26. *šú-gil niš-ïa mu-bi im*
Altogether there are twenty-five lines in the tablet.

šú-gil equals *napḫaru*, "what is collected", "totality", entirety". *šú* is a prefix to the causative stem (see on line 25). *gil* equals *paḫâru*, "collect".

niš-ĭa: the signs for the numerals twenty and five are the same as in Assyrian. *niš* is the Sumerian numeral for "twenty". *ĭa* is the Sumerian numeral for "five".

mu-bi im: *mu-bi* equals "his name", each line of the Hymn being considered a name of Bêl. In our translation we may read "its lines". *im*, the same sign as *nì* (line 1). *im* is sometimes equal to *ṭîṭu*, "clay", or *duppu*, "tablet"

27. *êr*(A.ŠI) *lim*(*b*)-*ma*
    Hymn of praise.

êr is a value derived from two signs, A and ŠI, taken together. The most common meaning of the value is *bikîtu*, "lamentation", or "song" (see *i-de*, line 6).

lim-ma: the phonetic complement *ma* indicates that the preceding value should end with *m*. Dr. Lau regards this as the sign *lib*(*m*) = *kûru* "woe", (Br. 7271); hence *êr-lim-ma* would mean a penitential psalm.

Chapter II

Tablet 13930, Plates 16 and 17, Hymn to Sin

Obverse

1. *mà-gur*(ḪAR) *azag an-na še-ir-ma-al nì*(IM)-*te-na*
   O shining ship of the heavens, majestic alone!

2. *a-a* *dimmer* *Šis-ki ù-mu-un-e Šis-unu-ki-ma*
   O father Nannar, lord of Ur!

3. *a-a* *dimmer* *Šis-ki ù-mu-un-e* È(BIT)-*ner-nu-gál*(IG)
   O father Nannar, lord of E-gišširgal!

4. *a-a* *dimmer* *Šis-ki ù-mu-un* *dimmer* *Áš-suḫ-ud*
   O father Nannar, lord of Namraṣit!

5. *ù-mu-un* *dimmer* *Šis-ki ṭu-mu sag* *dingir* *En-lil-lá*
   O lord Nannar, chief son of Bêl!

6. *síg*(DIRIG)-*ga-zu-ne síg*(DIRIG)-*ga-zu-ne*
   When thou art full, when thou art full,

7. *i-de*(NE) *a-a-zu i-de*(NE) *dimmer* *Mu-ul-lil-ra še-ir-ma-al-la-zu-ne*
   When before thy father, before Bêl thou art sovereign,

8. *a-a* ^{dimmer} *Šiš-*^{ki} *še-ir-ma-al-la-zu-ne gaba zi*(g)*-ga-zu-ne*
O father Nannar, when thou art sovereign, when thou liftest up the breast,

9. *mà-gur*(ḪAR) *an-šàg*(LIB)*-ga síg*(DIRIG)*-ga še-ir-ma-al-la-zu-ne*
O ship in the midst of the heavens, when thou art full and sovereign,

10. *a-a* ^{dimmer} *Šiš-*^{ki} *za-e éš*(AB) *azag-šù*(KU) *pa*(*d*)*-a-zu-ne*
O father Nannar, thou, when thou speakest to the shining house,

11. *a-a* ^{dimmer} *Šiš-*^{ki} *mà-dim êgâ*(A.MI.A) *síg*(DIRIG)*-ga-zu-ne*
O father Nannar, when like a ship on the tide thou art full,

12. *síg*(DIRIG)*-ga-zu-ne síg*(DIRIG)*-ga-zu-ne za-e síg*(DIRIG)*-ga-zu-ne*
When thou art full, when thou art full, thou, when thou art full,

13. *síg*(DIRIG)*-ga-zu-ne bi-šag-a-zu-ne za-e síg*(DIRIG)*-ga-zu-ne*
When thou art full, when thou speakest favorably, thou when thou art full,

14. *bi-šag-a rù*(UL)*-ti-a-zu-ne za-e síg*(DIRIG)*-ga-zu-ne*
When thou speakest graciously and engenderest life, thou, when thou art full!

15. *a-a* ^{dimmer} *Šiš-*^{ki} *lid damal lid-ne-ra sal-dug*(KA)*-ga-zu-ne*
O father Nannar of extensive progeny, when thou speakest to that progeny,

16. *a-a-zu ide*(ŠI) *ḫùl-la mu-e-ši-in-maš sal-zi ma-ra ni-in-gú*(KA)
Thy father discerns the joyful face and speaks life to the land.

17. *e i-i lugal-ra û*(*d*) (UD)*-de*(NE)*-eš e mu-un-ê*(UD.DU)
As an exalted royal command, daily he causes the word to go forth!

18. ^{dimmer} *Mu-ul-lil-li mu-du-ru û-sud-du šú-za ma-ra ni-in-rù*(UL)
Bel with the sceptre of distant days exalts thy hand over the land.

19. *Šiš-unu-*^{ki}*-ma mà-gur*(ḪAR) *azag-ga pa*(*d*)*-a-zu-ne*
When in Ur, O shining ship, thou speakest,

20. . . ^{dimmer} *Nu-dim-mud-e sal-dug*(KA)*-ga-zu-ne*
When to . . Ea thou speakest,

21. . . . . [*pa*(*d*)]*-a-zu*[*-ne*]
When . . . . . thou speakest,

Reverse

22. . . . .
. . . .

23. . . . . *lal a im*[*-si*]
. . . . with water is filled.

24. . . . . *gi a im-si*
. . . . with water is filled.

25. *ìd*(A.ṬÚ) . . . . *e a im-si* *dimmer* [*Šis-ki-kam*]
The river . . . . . . is filled with water by Nannar.

26. *azag-giìd*(A ṬÚ) *ud-kib-nun-na-ge*(KIT) *a im-si*[*dimmer Šis-ki-kam*]
The bright Euphrates is filled with water by Nannar.

27. *ìd*(A.ṬÚ) *nu e-bi làḫ-e a im-si* *dimmer* *Šis-ki-kam*
The empty river is filled with water by Nannar.

28. *sug maḫ sug ban*(TUR)-*da a im-si* *dimmer* *Šis-ki-kam*
The large marsh, the little marsh is filled with water by Nannar.

29. *êr*(A.ŠI) *lim*(LIB)-*ma* *dimmer* *En-zu*
Penitential Psalm to En-zu

This beautiful and interesting hymn begins with a picturesque and lordly epithet of the god whose full face so often shone upon the worshipper night by night. His fatherly nature and his full-orbed glory are dwelt upon in adoring and glowing terms. The name of his city and temple are mentioned. His power to lighten the world is acknowledged His peculiar relation of "son to Bêl" is announced. The phenomenon of his appearance in the heavens as the *full moon* is described to us from several points of view. This is the famous Nannar, dwelling in the temple of E-gišširgal at the ancient city of Ur. The sacred ship, becoming a peculiar emblem in Babylonian worship, symbolized several important ideas connected with Nannar's transit through the heavens by night or during the month. Perhaps Nannar was in the beginning a water-god. His power over the waters is graphically described.

Obverse

1. *mà-gur azag an-na še-ir-ma-al nì-te-na*
O shining ship of the heavens, majestic by thyself!

mà-gur is a boat of crescent form. Sin is a man sitting in the half circle of the moon and sailing across the firmament of the heavens as in a majestic ship. *mà*: the sign MÛ was originally pictorial and represented the rudder of the ship. The sign of our tablet is New-Babylonian and can be found in the inscriptions of Nebuchadrezzar II. It is half way between the old pictorial and the usual Assyrian MÛ. *gur*: the sign ḪAR probably refers to the body of the ship as "an enclosure", or more particularly to "the crescent form" of the ship, since ḪAR means "circular enclosure". The ḪAR of our text is much like the linear form found in the *Stèle des Vautours*.

azag equals *ellu*, "shining", (Br. 9890). The sign also has the value *ku* with the meaning *ellu*. *azag*, "shining", refers to the moon and the moon looks like a ship.

an-na (see Hymn to Bêl, line 18).

še-ir-ma-al nì-te-na (see Hymn to Bêl, line 1) The ideas of these two words find their way into the first line of the Ašurbânipal Hymn to Sin, K. 2861, (IV R. 9). *še-ir-ma-al* appears especially as *ner-gal* (*š-n* and *m-g*) and *nì-te-na* as *aš-ni maḫ-àm*; *e-diš-ši-šu ṣi-i-ru*.

2. *a-a* *dimmer* *Šis-*ki *ù-mu-un-e Šis-unu-*ki*-ma*
O father Nannar, lord of Ur!

a-a (see Hymn to Bêl, line 3)

dimmer *Šis-*ki is the most common Sumerian name of the god Sin, and means "brother of the land". Sin was probably looked upon as "the helper of earth". *dimmer* (see Hymn to Bêl, line 2). *Šis* equals *aḫu*, "brother", (Br. 6437). *ŠIŠ* sometimes has the value *uru*, especially when it means *naṣâru*, "keep". The *ŠIŠ* of our hymn is New-Babylonian, but is not essentially different from the *ŠIŠ* of Gudea. *ki* (see Hymn to Bêl, line 9).

ù-mu-un-e (see Hymn to Bêl, line 3).

*Šis-unu-*ki*-ma* means "of the brother's dwelling place". *Šis* means "brother". *unu* equals *šubtu*, "dwelling", (Br. 4792). *ma*, perhaps, can be taken as a sign of the genitive, being dialectic for *ga*, which is for *ge*, one of the values of KIT (see MSL. pp XI and XVI). Perhaps we ought to read this word *Uru-um-*ki*-ma*, taking the other value of ŠIŠ and also reading *um* instead of *unu*. In texts of OBI it would appear that UNU is closely related to UM as well as to AB.

3. *a-a* *dimmer* *Šis-*ki *ù-mu-un-e* È(BIT)-*ner-nu-gál*(IG)
O father Nannar, lord of E-gišširgal!

a-a *dimmer* *Šis-*ki *ù-mu-un-e* (see line 2).

È-ner-nu-gál is not the usual spelling. The more common form is *È-giš-šir-gal*. Our *È*(BIT)-*ner*(NER)-*nu*(NU)-*gál*(IG) which also occurs in Ḫammurabi (for example, in CH. Col. II, line 21, Plate II) is dialectic for *È*(BIT)-*giš*(IZ)-*šir*(ŠIR)-*gal*(GAL). *È*(BIT)-*giš*(IZ)-*šir*(ŠIR)-*gal*(GAL) is the spelling found in the Ašurbânipal Hymn. In the inscription of the Clay Cylinder of Nabonidus found at Ur (Col. I, line 30), the spelling is *È*(BIT)-*giš*(IZ)-*šir*(ŠIR)-*gal*-(GAL), but the margin has the spelling *È*(BIT)-*giš*(IZ)-*nu*(NU)-*gál*(IG). *È* equals *bîtu*, "house", (Br. 6238). *ner* evidently stands for *kiš*. These two values, *ner* and *kiš*, were represented by the same sign in old Babylonian; namely, PIRIĶĶU. From the sign PIRIĶĶU, there developed in Assyrian another sign, whose chief value is *kiš* with the meaning *kiššatu.* The sign here then should have the value *kiš*, or in old Babylonian *giš*, which is also one of the values of GISSU, a determinative before the name of a light. *nu* is for *šir* which equals *nûru*, "light". IṢ ŠIR is a common ideogram for "light". The interchange of NU and SIRU is not so easy to explain. The fact that NU instead of SIRU occurs in the name of the temple in the time of Hammurabi would go to show that the spelling of the word with NU is more primitive than the spelling with SIRU. Perhaps NU has a value *šir*. Brünnow recognizes the fact that NU in the name of the temple sometimes takes the place of SIRU (see Br. 2005 and 1657) There is a difference between IḲU and GALLU. IḲU equals *bašû*, while GALLU equals *rabû*. The *gal* (ES *mal*) of IḲU must be different from the *gal* of GALLU.

4. *a-a* ^dimmer^ *Šis-*^ki^ *ù-mu-un* ^dimmer^ *Áš-suḫ-ud*
O father Nannar, lord of Namraṣit!

a-a ^dimmer^ *Šis-*^ki^ *ù-mu-un* (see line 2).

^dimmer^ *Áš-suḫ-ud*. one of the citations Brünnow gives, in which the name of this god occurs, is in Incantation K. 3255 (IV R.² 2, 21), where, in the Sumerian as well as in the marginal reading of the Assyrian, Sin is said to be the lord of the god Namraṣit. ^dimmer^ *En-zu-na en* ^dimmer^ *Áš-suḫ-ud ra-ge* = ^ilu^ *Sin be-el Nam-ra-ṣi-it.* *Áš-suḫ-ud* means "the only foundation of light". *Áš* has a very common Assyrian equivalent *edu*, "one". *suḫ* equals *išdu*, "foundation", (Br. 4811). *ud* equals *urru*, "light", (see Br. 7798).

5 *ù-mu-un* ^dimmer^ *Šis-*^ki^ *ṭú-mu sag* ^dingir^ *En-lil-lá*
O lord Nannar, chief son of Bêl!

^dimmer^ *Šis-*^ki^ (see line 2).

ṭu-mu: ṬU.MU is a syllabic and dialectic form of DUMU (Br. 4069 and 11917). When DUMU stands for *mâru*, "son", it is supposed to have the value *du* (Br. 4081) *ṭu-mu* is no doubt for *dumu* and *du* is a shortened form of *dumu.* *ṭu*: the sign may be recognized as old Babylonian appearing in this form in the Code of Hammurabi (see also AL. p. 135, No. 328).

sag (see Hymn to Bêl, line 5). *ṭu-mu sag* must be equal to some such expression as "first born son", or "only begotten son".

^dingir^ *En-lil-lá*: in line 7, we shall have ^dimmer^ *Mu-ul-lil-ra* and in line 18, ^dimmer^ *Mu-ul-lil-li.* ^dingir^ may be preferred to ^dimmer^ because the sign is a determinative to an EK form. *En-lil-lá* consists of the god's name, *En-lil* (see *Mu-ul-lil* in Hymn to Bêl, line 2).

6. *síg-ga-zu-ne síg-ga-zu-ne*
When thou art full, when thou art full,

síg-ga-zu-ne is a *ḫal*-clause equal to *ina malîka*, "in thy fulness". *síg*: the sign to which this value is attached is composite. One element consists of SI whose chief meaning is "fill". The other element consists of A which means "water". SI.A then means "full of water", or "fulness". The sign, called DIRIGU, has two values ending with *g*; i. e., *dirig* related to the sign-name and *síg* which is quite certainly equal to *malû* (Br. 3722). *ga* is a phonetic complement (see Hymn to Bêl, line 4). *zu* is a determinate suffix of the second person (see Hymn to Bêl, line 21). *ne* is a postposition equal to *ina* (see Br. 4602, also *de* in Hymn to Bêl, line 6).

7. *i-de a-a-zu i-de* *dimmer* *Mu-ul-lil-ra še-ir-ma-al-la-zu-ne*
When before thy father, before Bêl thou art sovereign,

i-de (see Hymn to Bêl, line 6). *i-de* is a preposition used as a noun in the construct state, having the meaning of *maḫru* or *pânu* and equal to *ina maḫar* or *ina pân*.

a-a-zu equals noun *a-a*, plus suffix *zu*. *a-a* (see Hymn to Bêl, line 3). *zu* (see line 6).

dimmer *Mu-ul-lil-ra* equals god's name *dimmer* *Mu-ul-lil*, plus phonetic complement *ra*. *dimmer* *Mu-ul-lil* (see Hymn to Bêl, line 2). *ra* (see Hymn to Bêl, line 3). It might be better to regard *lil-ra* as a shortened form of *lil-lá-ra*. *lil* is quite apt to take the phonetic complement *lá*, a value of the sign LALLU, while *ra* is naturally a postposition.

še-ir-ma-al-la-zu-ne is a *ḫal*-clause equal to "in thy sovereignty". *še-ir-ma-al* (see Hymn to Bêl, line 1) *zu-ne* (see line 6).

8. *a-a* *dimmer* *Šis-ki* *še-ir-ma-al-la-zu-ne gaba zi-ga-zu-ne*
O father Nannar, when thou art sovereign, when thou liftest up thy breast,

a-a *dimmer* *Šis-ki* (see line 2).

še-ir-ma-al-la-zu-ne (see line 7).

gaba equals *irtu*, "breast", (Br. 4470). We have had *gaba* as an adjective equal to *pitû* (see Hymn to Bêl, line 6).

zi-ga-zu-ne is a *ḫal*-clause meaning "in thy lifting up". *zi* equals *našû*, "lift up", (Br. 2325). We have had *zi* as equal to *kênu*, "right", and *napištu*, "life", (see Hymn to Bêl, lines 4 and 25). *ga* is a phonetic complement. *zi* might be *zig* (see Br. 2303 and Hymn to Bêl, line 4). *zu-ne* (see line 6). In *gaba zi-ga-zu-ne*, perhaps we have the picture of the full moon suddenly rising in the night from the horizon

9. *mà-gur an-šàg-ga síg-ga še-ir-ma-al-la-zu-ne*
O ship in the midst of the heavens, when thou art full and sovereign,

mà-gur (see line 1).

an-šàg-ga: ŠÂGU is usually taken as a preposition and stands before its object. Here it seems to follow its object, *an* (see Hymn to Bêl, line 18). *šàg-ga* equals LIB plus GA. *šàg*: ŠÂGU, equal to *libbu*, may have either one of three values; viz., *šà* when not followed by a phonetic complement, *šàg* when followed by the phonetic complement *ga* and *šàb* when followed by the phonetic complement *ba* (see Br. 7980 and Hymn to Bêl, line 22). *ga* (see Hymn to Bêl, line 4).

síg-ga (see line 6).

še-ir-ma-al-la-zu-ne (see line 7).

10. *a-a* dimmer *Šis-*ki *za-e éš azag-šù pa(d)-a-zu-ne*

O father Nannar, thou, when thou speakest to the shining house,

a-a dimmer *Šis-*ki (see line 2).

za-e (see Hymn to Bêl, line 16).

éš (see Hymn to Bêl, line 16). *éš* is admittedly a Sumerian value as is shown by its relation to the sign-name ÊŠU. *éš* is the fuller form of è(BIT). From *éš* there has arisen a Semitic loan-word *ešu*, "house".

azag-šù means "to the shining". *azag* (see line 1). *šù* (see Hymn to Bêl, line 15).

pa(d)-a-zu-ne is a *ḫal*-clause composed of a preposition with an infinitive that governs a suffix, as *ina tamîka*, "in thy speaking", i. e., "when thou speakest". *pad* is a verb equal to *tamû*, "speak". *pad* also equals *zakâru*, "to name". *pa*, the shortened form of *pad*, evidently intended here, is sometimes represented by the Assyrian *nabû*. *a* is the vowel of prolongation indicating the *pa*, rather than the *pad*-value. *zu-ne* (see line 6).

11. *a-a* dimmer *Šis-*ki *mà-dim êgâ síg-ga-zu-ne*

O father Nannar, when like a ship on the tide thou art full,

a-a dimmer *Šis-*ki (see line 2).

mà-dim consists of noun *mà* and postposition *dim*. *mà* (see on line 1) *mà-gur* refers to the moon. *mà* refers to an ordinary ship *dim* is equal to *kîma*, "like". The sign-name is DIMMU. *dim* is ES. The EK form of the value is *gim*.

êgâ is a contraction of *a*, *gè* and *a* from the signs A, MI and A, and means "tide", or "high water". *a* means "water" and MI with the value *gè* means "black", and the second A is evidently phonetic only. *êgâ*, therefore, means "black water", such water as is seen in a "flood" or "high tide".

síg-ga-zu-ne (see line 6).

12. *síg-ga-zu-ne síg-ga-zu-ne za-e síg-ga-zu-ne*
When thou art full, when thou art full, thou, when thou art full,

síg-ga-zu-ne (see line 6).

za-e (see line 10). It may be noticed that *síg-ga-zu-ne* occurs three times in this line and ten times in the section, lines 6—18. This repetition no doubt serves for rhetorical effect, especially in oral delivery and, together with the marked uniformity of measure in the clauses, characterizes the passage as poetic.

13. *síg-ga-zu-ne bi-šag-a-zu-ne za-e síg-ga-zu-ne*
When thou art full, when thou speakest favorably, thou, when thou art full,

síg-ga-zu-ne (see line 6).

bi-šag-a-zu-ne is a *ḫal*-clause equal to "in thy speaking graciously". *bi* equals *ḳibû*, "speak", (Br. 5124). Starting with the meaning "speak" the sign KÂŠU comes to have a demonstrative force and is generally used as a suffix of the third person singular. We shall also see that it sometimes equals *šikaru* "strong drink". *šag*: the sign giving this value is one not much used. It may be identified as GIŠIMMAR (see AL. p. 130, No. 206, also Br. 7286). *šag* is the chief value, equal to *damâḳu* or *damḳu*, "gracious". *a*: the value is generally followed by the phonetic complement *ga*, but here it is followed by *a* (see Hymn to Bêl, line 9). *zu-ne* (see line 6).

14. *bi-šag-a rù-ti-a-zu-ne za-e síg-ga-zu-ne*
When thou speakest graciously and engenderest life, thou, when thou art full,

bi-šag-a (see line 13).

rù-ti-a-zu ne is a *ḫal*-clause equal to "in thy engendering life". *rù*: we have had UL already as a composite part of *Mu-ul-lil* (see Hymn to Bêl, line 2). UL here probably with the value *rù* equals *kalâlu*, "perfect". The sign is intended to be the picture of a goring bull; then, as we get away from the primary idea, there arise the meanings of "exultation", "perfection", etc. Nannar is "the perfecter of life". *ti* (see Hymn to Bêl, line 16). *a* (see Hymn to Bêl, line 9). *zu-ne* (see line 6).

za-e (see line 10).

síg-ga-zu-ne (see line 6).

15. *a-a* *dimmer* *Šis-ki* *lid damal lid-ne-ra sal-dug-ga-zu-ne*
O father Nannar of extensive progeny, when thou speakest to that progeny,

a-a *dimmer* *Šis-ki* (see on line 2).

lid may be of Semitic origin from the Assyrian word *littu*, "progeny". The two horizontal lines in the sign suggest the idea of "pairing", from which comes the idea of "progeny" (thus, Prince, MSL., p. 223).

damal (see Hymn to Bêl, line 10).

lid-ne-ra equals "to that progeny". *ne* equals *annû*, a demonstrative pronoun "this". *ne* is cognate with *de* which is also cognate with *da* and *ta* used as postpositions (see *de* and *da* in Hymn to Bêl, lines 6 and 4). *ra* is a postposition = "unto" (see Hymn to Bêl, line 3).

sal-dug-ga-zu-ne is a *ḥal*-clause: "in thy speaking". *sal* is a prefix of an abstract character. It is equivalent to the Assyrian *zinništu*, "feminine". It is a counterpart to *ku* in the expressions *Eme-sal* and *Eme-ku*, *ku* being equal to *bêlu*, "lord". As a prefix, *sal* generalizes the root-idea of the stem to which it is attached and is consequently an abstract prefix (see Br. 10930, 10949 and 10955). *dug-ga* (see Hymn to Bêl, line 4). *zu-ne* (see line 6)

16. *a-a-zu ide ḥùl-la mu-e-ši-in-maš sal-zi ma-ra ni-in-gú*
Thy father discerns the joyful face and speaks life to the land.

a-a-zu (see on line 7).

ide equals *pânu*, "face", (Br. 9281). The sign IGÛ can be read either *ide*, which is ES, or *ige*, which is EK.

ḥùl-la equals noun *ḥùl*, plus phonetic complement *la*. *ḥùl* equals *ḥadû*, "joy" (Br. 10884). The sign giving this value is not to be confounded with another sign which also has the value *ḥul* meaning "evil", expressed by *limuttu* (Br. 9503).

mu-e-ši-in-maš is a verb consisting of verbal prefix *mu*, verbal infixes *e* and *ši-in* and root *maš*. *mu* (see Hymn to Bêl, lines 1 and 18). *e* (see Hymn to Bêl, line 18). *ši-in*: an objective verbal infix naturally has its person determined by the object to which it refers. That object in this case seems to be *ide ḥul-la*, "the joyful face" of the moon. *maš*: the sign has two names, BÂRU and MÂŠU, and two chief values related to these names, *bar* and *maš*. *bar* and *maš* are cognate forms. *b* changes to *m* (MSL. p. X); *r* changes to *š* (MSL. p. XII). The sign has two chief meanings, "side" and "cut". The meaning of "side" is represented by *bar* (see MSL. p. 234), while the meaning of "cut", from which we get the idea of "distinguish" is generally represented by the value *maš* (Br. 1735).

sal-zi consists of abstract prefix *sal* and noun *zi*. *sal* (see on line 15). *zi* (see on line 8).

ma-ra equals "unto the land". *ma* (see Hymn to Bêl, line 8). *ra* (see line 15).

ni-in-gú: *ni* can be a verbal prefix and *in* a verbal infix, or *ni-in* can be a verbal infix with the verbal prefix omitted, *gú* being the verbal root. *ni*, if taken as a prefix, naturally refers to *a-a-zu*. *ni* may have a demonstrative force, equal to *šuatu*, like *ne*. *in* as an infix refers to *ma-ra*. *gú*, a shortened form of *gug*, equal either *ḳibû*, "speak", or *apâlu*, "answer". *gú* and *gug* have dialectic forms *du* and *dug*, the *g* changing to *d* which ES prefers The sign is apparently a modification of the sign SANGU (see AL p. 121, No. 14, and p. 124, No. 87). The primary meaning was "opening" and the leading value is *ka* equal to *pû*, "mouth". The values *ka* and *gú* come from the sign-name KÂGU (see Hymn to Bêl, lines 1 and 4). With the value *ì* the sig means "word".

17. *e i-i lugal-ra û-de-eš e mu-un-ê*
   As an exalted royal command, daily he causes the word to go forth!

e (see Hymn to Bêl, line 14).

i-i: *i* is the chief value of GIṬṬÛ. The sign with its five parallel lines or wedges representing the five fingers of the hand is a symbol of power. From the idea of "power", we get that of "exaltation" (see Hymn to Bêl, line 6).

lugal-ra consists of stem *lugal* and postposition *ra*. *lugal*: the sign is composite, the elements being GAL and LU which mean "great" and "man". *lugal* equals *šarru* (Br. 4266). We shall have the element LU with the ES value *mulu*. *ra* (see Hymn to Bêl, lines 8 and 8). We might expect *la* here.

û-de-eš consists of root *û*, phonetic complement *de* and adverbial ending *eš*. *û* equals *ûmu*, "day", (Br. 7797), and is a shortened form of *ud*. *de* is phonetic here. The more usual phonetic complement of *ud* is *da* (see Br. 7774). *eš* (see Br. 10001). *eš* as an adverbial ending is probably derived from the Semitic adverbial ending *-iš* which is supposed to have grown out of the Assyrian suffix of the third person *šu*. Agglutinative languages do not often possess special adverbial endings.

mu-un-ê consists of verbal prefix *mu-un* and verbal root *ê*. *mu-un* is phonetic for *mun* which is simply a nasalized *mu* (see MSL. p. XXVIII, and Hymn to Bêl, line 1). On *ê* (see Hymn to Bêl, line 15).

18. *dimmer Mu-ul-lil-li mu-du-ru û-sud-du šú-za ma-ra ni-in-rù*
   Bêl with the sceptre of distant days exalts thy hand over the land.

dimmer Mu-ul-lil-li (see Hymn to Bêl, line 23).

mu-du-ru: there is a sign MUDRU (Br. 10776) which may be related to PA. We may infer a relation between MUDRU and PA, because the two signs have a common value *sig*. We know also that MU.DU.RU sometimes stands for PA (Br. 1275). Now if MU.DU.RU can stand for PA it must have some meaning in common with PA. The most usual meaning of PA is *ḫaṭṭu*, "sceptre", which gives good sense here. *mu* (see Hymn to Bêl, line 1). *du* (see Hymn to Bêl, line 15).

û-sud-du consists of noun *û*, adjective *sud*, and phonetic complement *du*. *û* (see line 17). *sud* equals *rûḳu*, "distant" (Br. 7603). *du* (see *gin*, line 23), phonetic complement here.

šú-za equals noun *šú* and suffix *za*. *šú* (see Hymn to Bêl, line 25). *za* is a suffix of the second person singular masculine (Br. 11722). We have had *za-e* as being equal to "thou" (Hymn to Bêl, line 16). *zu* we have found to be the more usual suffix of the second person (see on line 6). *za* is dialectic for *zu*.

ma-ra (see on line 16).

ni-in-rù consists of prefix *ni*, infix *in* and verbal root *rù*. *ni-in* (see on line 16). *rù* (see on line 14).

19. *Šis-unu-*[ki]*-ma mà-gur azag-ga pa(d)-a-zu-ne*
When in Ur, O shining ship, thou speakest,

Šis-unu-[ki]*-ma* (see on line 2).

mà-gur (see on line 1).

azag-ga equals adjective *azag*, plus phonetic complement *ga*. *azag* (see on line 1). *ga* (see Hymn to Bêl, line 4).

pa(d)-a-zu-ne (see on line 10).

20. . . [dimmer] *Nu-dim-mud-e sal-dug-ga-zu-ne*
When to . . Ea thou speakest,

[dimmer] *Nu-dim-mud-e*: we have here a compound ideogram as a name of the god Ea. [dimmer] is the determinative before the name of a god (see Hymn to Bêl, line 2). *Nu-dim-mud* equals the Assyrian E-a (Br. 2016). The usual Sumerian ideogram is EN.KI. *e* in *Nu-dim-mud-e* a vowel of prolongation (see Hymn to Bêl, line 3).

sal-dug-ga-zu-ne (see line 15).

21. . . . . [*pa(d)*]*-a-zu*[*-ne*]
When . . . . . thou speakest,

pa(d)-a-zu-ne (see line 10).

Reverse

22. . . . .

23. . . . . . *la a im*[*-si*]
. . . . with water is filled

a equals *mû*, "water" (Br. 11347). "Water" is a primary meaning of the sign ÂU, which at first consisted of two short perpendicular lines representing "falling water" (see Hymn to Bêl, line 3).

im-si consists of indeterminate verbal prefix *im* and verbal root *si*. *im* (Br. p. 545). *si* (Hymn to Bêl, line 22).

24. . . . . *gi a im-si*
. . . . . with water is filled.

a im-si (see line 23).

25. *id* . . . . . . *e a im-si* [dimmer] [*Šis-ki-kam*]
The river . . . . is filled with water by Nannar.

id equals *nâru*, "river". Sometimes *id* is shortened to *i* (Br. 11647). The value *id* comes from the union of two signs A „water" and ṬÚ (Br. 10217). Moreover, ṬÚ with the value *ṭú* equals *apsû*, "sea". The ṬÚ sign, explained more minutely, consists of ḪAL "run" inside of KIL "enclosure". So ḪAL + KIL = "running, flowing within an enclosure", hence = "sea". While *id* means primarily "water of the sea", it is much used also as a determinative before names of rivers. We have the name of the Euphrates in the next line. Perhaps the name of the Tigris was given in some one of the lines. The common Sumerian ideogram for the name of the Tigris is *ḫal-ḫal*, an intensified form of *ḫal*, which means "running" or "rushing". The Tigris is thus very appropriately called "the rushing river". The Babylonian *Diglat* in the hands of the Persians took the form *Tigra*.

26. *azag-gi id ud-kib-nun-na-ge a im-si* [[dimmer] *Šis-ki-kam*]
The bright Euphrates is filled with water by Nannar.

azag-gi equals *ellu*, "shining" (Br. 9901). *azag* (see line 19). *gi* is a phonetic complement, chosen no doubt with a view to vowel harmony as regards the following *id* (?). GI as an ideogram means "reed" (see Hymn to Bêl, line 24, *gin*).

[id] *ud-kib-nun-na-ge* means the river of Sippar. For *id*, see on line 25. *ud-kib-nun* consists of *ud* "sun" + *kib* "flourish, generate", and *nun* "great". The sign KIB suggests the idea "double" and hence, of course, "generate, beget" (MSL. p. 203). *Nun*, of course, = *rabû* "great" (Br. 2628), while *na* must be the phonetic complement and *ge* the *nota genitivi* as used in the next Hymn. The form *ud-kib-nun* then seems to mean "the great (*nun*) generative force (*kib*) of the sun" (*ud*); a name applied to Sippar had been from time immemorial the seat of the worship of the sun-god Šamaš (RBA., pp. 69, 117). *Id-ud-kib-nun-na-ge* then simply means "the river (*id*) of (*ge*) Sippar", viz., the Euphrates,

which was usually termed in Sumerian *Bura-nunu* "the great stream" (MSL. p. 7, C).

a im-si (see on line 23).

27. *ìd nu e-bi láḫ-e a im-si* dimmer *Šis-*ki*-kam*
The empty river is filled with water by Nannar.

ìd (see on line 25).

nu, regular Sumerian negative abverb, equal to the Assyrian *la*.

e-bi equals noun *e* and suffix *bi*. *e* equals *mû*, "water" (Br. 5844). We have also had *e* equal to *ḳabû*, "speech" (Hymn to Bêl, line 14). *bi* is a suffix of the third person singualar (see Br. 5135). *bi* gets its demonstrative nature from the conception "speak" which seems to be the primary one in the old Babylonian linear hieroglyph.

láḫ-e consists of root *láḫ* and vocalic prolongation *e*. *láḫ* equals *misû* "wash" (Br. 6167). It is used of washing the hands and feet. It gets the idea "wash" from the idea "servant" who does the washing, but it may have meant "servant" before it meant "wash". It often has the phonetic complement *ḫa* or *ḫi*. Literally the clause read : "the river whose water washes not".

a im-si (see on line 23).

dimmer *Šis-*ki*-kam* equals god-name dimmer *Šis-*ki plus *kam* = KAMMU without doubt (see CT. XV, Colophon of Tablet 29623, plate 12). *kam* is a well recognized determinative used after ordinal numerals. It no doubt occupies this position as a genitive particle, but, as a genitive sign, it may be used after words other than numerals; and, in fact, is so used in Gudea. It is evidently a lengthened form of the postposition *ka*, being *ka* plus *am* (see SVA. p 60).

28. *sug maḫ sug ban-da a im-si* dimmer *Šis-*ki*-kam*
The great marsh, the little marsh is filled with water by Nannar.

The sign looks like MÀ but perhaps the copyist made a mistake.

maḫ (see Hymn to Bêl, line 23).

sug equals *ṣuṣû*, "marsh". The sign is the enclosure-sign KIL with the "water" sign ÂU within the "enclosure" sign.

ban-da: the signs are DUMU and DADDU. DUMU has several values, the chief of which are *dumu*, *tur* and *ban*. *dumu* equals *mâru*, "son". We have met the value *dumu* or its dialectic equivalent *ṭumu*, represented by ṬU and MU (see on line 5). *tur* equals *ṣiḫru*, "small", and is naturally followed by the phonetic complement *ra*. *ban-da* also equals *ṣiḫru* "little" (Br. 4133).

a im-si (see on line 23).

dimmer *Šis-*ki*-kam* (see line 27).

29. *êr lim-ma dimmer En-zu*
Penitential Psalm to Sin.

êr-lim-ma (see Hymn to Bêl, line 27).

dimmer En-zu "lord of wisdom" is the other name by which Sin is known in Sumerian. We have had one name above; viz., *dimmer Šiš-ki*. *dimmer En-zu* is no doubt in genitive relation to the preceding part of the line, although the *nota genitivi* is lacking. In another hymn to Bêl (CT. XV, Tablet 29644, plate 12), the genitive relation is signified by the postposition *kam*. The words are: *êr-lim-ma dingir En-lil-lá-kam.*

Chapter III

Tablet 29631, Plates 15 and 16, Hymn To ADAD

Obverse

1. [*ḫad*-]*ê*(UD.DU)-*a mu-zu an*[-*zak-ku*]
In the lightning flash thou proclaimest thy name.

2. *dimmer Mer*(IM) *bi-maḫ ḫad-ê*(UD.DU)-*a mu-zu an*[-*zak-ku*]
O Adad, in the mighty thunder and the lightning flash thou declarest thy name.

3. [*dimmer*] *Mer*(IM) *dumu An-na bi-maḫ ḫad-ê*(UD.DU)-*a mu-zu an-za*[*k-ku*]
O Adad, son of Anu, in the mighty thunder and the lightning flash thou declarest thy name.

4. *ù-mu-un nì*(IM)-*ki-ge*(KIT) *bi-maḫ ḫad-ê*(UD.DU)-*a mu-zu an-zak*[-*ku*]
O lord, dread of earth, in the mighty thunder and the lightning flash thou declarest thy name.

5. *dimmer Mer*(IM) *ù-mu-un ib*(TUM)-*mal*(IG)-*la bi-maḫ ḫad-ê*-(UD.DU)-*a mu-zu an*[-*zak-ku*]
O Adad, lord of great wrath, in the mighty thunder and the lightning flash thou declarest thy name.

6. *bar*(*maš*?)-*tab-ba ù-mu-un dimmer ama-an-ki-ga bi-maḫ ḫad-ê* (UD.DU)-*a* [*mu-zu an-zak-ku*]
O twin, lord, bull-god of heaven and earth, in the mighty thunder and the lightning flash thou declarest thy name.

7. *a-a dimmer Mer*(IM) *ù-mu-un ud-da bar-ru-a mu-zu an-zak-ku*
O father ADAD, lord, when the light is darkened thou declarest thy name.

8. *a-a* dimmer *Mer*(IM) *û*(UD)-*gal-la bar-ru-a mu-zu an-zak-ku*
O father Adad, when the great day is darkened thou declarest thy name.

9. *a-a* dimmer *Mer*(IM) *uku*(UG)-*gal-la bar-ru-a mu-zu an-zak-ku*
O father Adad, when the great king is cut off thou declarest thy name.

10. dimmer *Mer*(IM) *uku*(UG) *An-na bi-maḫ ḫad-ê*(UD.DU)-*a mu-zu an-zak-ku*
O Adad, king of Anu, in the mighty thunder and the lightning flash thou declarest thy name.

11. *mu-zu kalam*(UN)-*ma mu-un-rù*(UL)-*rù*(UL)-*rù*(UL)
Thy name is mightily magnificent in the earth.

12. *me-lam*(NE)-*zu kalam*(UN)-*ma tug*(KU)-*gim im-mi-in-dul*
Thy brightness covers the land like a garment.

13. *za ḫad*(PA) *aka*(RAM)-*zu-šù*(KU) *kur-gal a-a* dimmer *Mu-ul-lil sag im-da-sig*(PA)-*gi*
The lightning of thy thunder smites the head of the great mountain, father Bêl.

14. *urša*(ḪAR.DU)-*zu àma*(DAGAL) *gal* dimmer *Nin-lil ba-e-di-ḫu-láḫ-e*
Thy thunder terrifies the great mother Belit.

15. dingir *En-lil-li dumu-ni* dimmer *Mer*(IM)-*ra à*(ID) *mu-un-da-an-aka*(RAM)
Bêl to his son Adad measures out power.

16. *mulu dumu-mu û*(UD) *um-me-ši-si-si û*(UD) *um-me-ši-lá-lá*
Thou who art my son, the day thou didst lift up the eye, the day thou didst look!

17. dimmer *Mer*(IM)-*ri û*(UD) *um-me-ši-si-si û*(UD) *um-me-ši-lá-lá*
O Adad, the day thou didst lift up the eye, the day thou didst look!

18. *û*(UD) *iminna-bi-meš ba-gan-tal*(RI)-*lá û*(UD) *um-me-ši-lá-lá*
During seven days thou didst blow a full blast when thou didst look.

19. *û*(UD) *ì*(KA) *di-zu-ka ḫàr*(GUD)-*ḫa-ra ab-ba û*(UD) *um-me-ši-lá-lá*
It was the day of the word of the word of thy judgment, O bull-god of the abyss, the day thou didst look.

20. *nim-gir luḫ su-ši-šù*(KU) *mu-ra-du-ud*
As the lightning, the messenger of terror, thou didst go.

21. *mulu dumu-mu rù*(UL) *gin*(DU)*-na-gin*(DU)*-na a-ba zi-gi-en te-ga*(BA)
When thou who art my son goest violently about, who can attack like thee!

Reverse

22. *ki-bala ḫul gíg a-a muḫ-zu-šù*(KU) *a-ba za-e-gim te-ga*(BA)
The troublesome evil hostile land, O father, which is against thee; who like thee can attack!

23. *ná*(DAḲ) *imi tur-tur-e šú-um-me-ti a-ba za-e-gim te-ga*(BA)
The little stone of the storm do thou take! Who can attack like thee!

24. *ná*(DAḲ) *gal-gal-e šú-um-me-ti a-ba za-e-gim te-ga*(BA)
The large stone do thou take! Who can attack like thee!

25. *ná*(DAḲ) *tur-tur-zu ná*(DAḲ) *gal-gal-zu muḫ-ba ù-me-dm*(A.AN)
Thy little stone, thy large stone, on it (the land) it lieth!

26. *ki-bala-a zi-da-zu ù-mu-e-gul da bur*(BU) *su ù-mu-e-se*
The hostile land thy right hand destroys. It gives powerful bodily destruction (?)

27. *dimmer Mer*(IM)*-ri dug*(KA)*-dug*(KA)*-ga a-a muḫ-na-šù*(KU) *geš* (IZ)*-ni ba-ši-in-ag*
Adad, when he speaks (to one), O father, on him he imposes his government.

28. *a-a dimmer Mer*(IM) *è*(BIT)*-ta ê*(UD.DU)*-a-ni û*(UD) *ì*(KA) *di na-nam*
Father Adad, when he comes out of the house, he fixes the day of judgment.

29. *è*(BIT)*-ta eri-ta ê*(UD DU)*-a-ni uku*(UG) *ban*(TUR)*-da na-nam*
When he comes out of the house or out of the city, he fixes the great day,

30. *eri-ta an-na-ta gar*(ŠÂ)*-ra-ni û*(UD) *ì*(KA)*-ḫar-ra na-nam*
When he establishes himself out of the city out of heaven, he fixes the day of curse.

31. . . . *êr*(A.ŠI) *lim*(LIB)*-ma dimmer Mer*(IM)
. . . . . Hymn to Adad.

This hymn we find to be full of action. The lightning flashes in the first line, and we see at least three distinct kinds of storm placed on the scene, one succeeding the other. The thunder storm first passes over our head. We see the lightning, we hear the roar of the thunder, the earth is placed in fear, the day turns dark, the top of the mountain is smitten, the very gods themselves are terrified. Secondly comes the flood. The storm of the hour is lengthened into one of days. It becomes a deluge of judgment on the earth. The words say seven days, but in such poetic discourse seven might perhaps simply mean "many". Finally, there is a decided change in the scene. The flood has passed away. The death-destroying hail-storm falls upon us, not simply the little hail-stones, but the great hail-stones. The day, of course, has come.

But the effects of Adad's power so artistically set forth in this hymn are secondary, as placed beside the dignity of the god himself. The word of Adad is absolute and all-powerful. He is a god of great wrath. He is a real bull-god, of heaven and earth. He can put the heavens out of sight He can make day as black as the darkest night. He can split the earth with his lightning. He can flood the land with water. He can pelt its inhabitants with stones. Yet in all this he consults with father Bêl.

Obverse

1. [*ḫad*]-*ê-a mu-zu an*-[*zak-ku*]
   In the lightning flash thou proclaimest thy name!

ḫad-ê-a is a *ḫal*-clause, consisting of noun *ḫad*, participle *ê* and postposition *a*, and means "in the going out of the sceptre", or freely, "in the lightning flash". The apodosis is *mu-zu an-zak-ku*. *ḫad* (PA) equals *ḫaṭṭu*, "sceptre" (Br. 5573). The value *ḫad* may be of Semitic origin, but note that its cognate *ḫud* is equal to *namâru*, "brightness" (Br. 5582), as is also *kun*, another value of PA "staff"; then PA = "a lighted torch". *ê* we have had as equal to *aṣû* (Hymn to Bêl, line 15). *ê* is also equal to *šûpû*, "flashing" (Br. 5638). *a* equals *ina*, "in" (Br. 11365).

mu-zu means "thy name". *mu* equals *šumu*, "name" (Br. 1235).

an-zak-ku is a verb. *an* is an indeterminate verbal prefix. The context shows it to be of the second person (see MSL. p. XXVI). *zak-ku* may mean "utter a decree" (Br. 6519). For example, *zak* equals *tamîtu*, "a decree" (Br. 6493). Perhaps it could as well be a verb signifying "to decree", or "to establish". *ku* also equals *tamû*, "utter" (Br. 10555), but it would be simpler to make *ku* a phonetic complement to *zak*. It may be that we ought to read the clause: "thy name utters the decree". But "thy name" has the usual position of the object. It is also rather awkward to regard *zak* as an object placed between the verbal prefix and the verb.

2. *dimmer Mer bi-maḫ ḫad-ê-a mu-zu an*-[*zak-ku*]
   O Adad, in the mighty thunder and the lightning flash thou declarest thy name.

dimmer Mer: this is the Sumerian name of the storm-god. *Mer* being one of the values of the sign IMMU. The fact that the sign in some cases in this hymn (e. g. lines 15 and 17) is followed by the phonetic complement *ri* or *ra* shows that *Mer* is the value intended for the name of the god *Mer* is probably from *imi* changed to *immer* and then to *Mer* and hence, like *imi*, means "wind" and "storm". The name *Mer* offers no suggestion as to the origin of the Semitic names *Rammânu* and *Addu*.

bi-maḫ equals "mighty utterance". *bi* (see Hymn to Sin, line 13). *maḫ* (see Hymn to Bêl, line 23).

ḫad-ê-a mu-zu an-zak-ku (see on line 1).

3. [*dimmer*] *Mer dumu An-na bi-maḫ ḫad-ê-a mu-zu an-za*[*k-ku*]
O Adad, son of Anu, in the mighty thunder and the lightning flash thou declarest thy name.

dumu (see Hymn to Sin, line 5, *ṭu-mu*).

An-na, ideogram for the god of heaven, plus phonetic complement. Note that AN for the god Anu does not take the determinative god sign. Probably the omission is due to the desire to avoid the occurrence of AN twice in succession. It must have been after Adad had taken the place of Ištar in the second triad of gods that Adad was called the son of Anu. The earlier arrangement was Anu, Bêl, Ea, Sin, Šamaš and Ištar. The later order was Anu, Bêl and Ea, as rulers of the universe, and Sin, Šamaš and Adad, as rulers of heaven under the command of Anu. This new grouping was the result of a theological development. Ištar was found to be one of the planets, and, therefore, not to be classed longer along with Sin and Šamaš Adad, the god of the atmosphere, was thought to be a personality of sufficient dignity to take the place formerly occupied by Ištar.

bi-maḫ ḫad-ê-a mu-zu an-zak-ku (see on lines 1 and 2).

4. *ù-mu-un ni-ki-ge bi-maḫ ḫad-ê-a mu-zu an-zak-*[*ku*]
O lord, dread of earth, in the mighty thunder and the lightning flash thou declarest thy name.

ù-mu-un (see Hymn to Bêl, line 1).

ni-ki-ge. *ni* is a value of IMMU equal to *puluḫtu*, "fear" (see Hymn to Bêl, line 18). *ki* equals *irṣitu*, "earth" (see Hymn to Bêl, line 9). *ge* is a postpositive sign of the genitive (see Br. 5935.

bi-maḫ ḫad-ê-a mu-zu an-zak-ku (see lines 1 and 2).

5. *dimmer Mer ù-mu-un ib-mal-la bi-maḫ ḫad-ê-a mu-zu an-*[*zak-ku*]
O Adad, lord of great wrath, in the mighty thunder and and the lightning flash thou declarest thy name.

ib-mal-la: *ib* is a value of TUM equal to *agâgu*, "anger" (Br. 4954). *mal* is a value of IḲU which is dialectic for PISANNU and also for MA.AL (see Hymn to Bêl, lines 1 and 18, and Hymn to Sin, 2). *ib-mal* = "wrathful" (Br. 2242).

bi-maḫ ḫad-ê-a mu-zu an-zak-ku (see on lines 1 and 2).

6. *tab-tab-ba ù-mu-un dimmer ama-an-ki-ga bi-maḫ ḫad-ê-a* [*mu-zu an-zak-ku*]

O twin, lord, bull-god of heaven and earth, in the mighty thunder and the lightning flash thou declarest thy name.

bar-tab-ba equals *tu'âmu*, "twin" (Br. 1896). *maš* equals *tu'âmu* (Br. 1811), while the cognate *bar* equals *tappû*, "companion" (Br. 1807) *maš*, which represents the idea "cut", is more primitive than *bar* which represents the idea "side". *maš* is also equal to *mâšu*, "twin", a Sumerian loan-word in Assyrian. *tab* equals *tappû* (Br. 3775). *tab* may have been inserted, that *bar* "companion" should be taken rather than the narrower word "twin" (Hymn to Sin, 16). *ba* is a phonetic complement (Br 102 and Hymn to Bêl, line 25). Adad is called "twin" or "companion", because he possessed a composite nature, comprising in himself the elements of several gods. The manifestations of power seen in wind and rain and in lightning and thunder, would logically lead to the conclusion that his nature was divided, or that he brought to his aid several gods endowed with powers suited to different kinds of effort. The gods that aided Adad were sometimes looked upon as birds, one of whom was the god Zû, who presided over the tempest. Zû's mother mother was Siris, lady of the rain and clouds. Then there was Martu, the lord of the squall, and Barḳu, the genius of the lightning. The son of Zû was a strong bull who pastured in the meadows, bringing abundance and fertility. There was also Šûtu, the south wind. He, no doubt, was an agent of Adad's. There is another way in which Adad may be looked upon as twin-like in his nature. He could pass suddenly from the fiercest anger to gentlest kindness. He was represented in sculpture as carrying a battle-axe. Kings invoked his aid against their enemies. In his passionate rage he destroyed everything before him. When his wrath was appeased, however, there might come the gentle breeze and the refreshing shower. The fields which he had devastated he also caused to blossom and produce fruit and grain

dimmer (see Hymn to Bêl, line 2).

ama-an-ki-ga: *ama* equals *rîmu*, "bull" (see Hymn to Bêl, line 7 and 9). *an* (see Hymn to Bêl, line 18). *ki* (see on line 4). *ga* seems to be a postposition (see MSL. p. XVI). *ga* might perhaps be equal to *bašû*, "being" (Br. 6109).

bi-maḫ ḫad-e-a mu-zu an-zak-ku (see on lines 1 and 2).

7. *a-a* *dimmer* *Mer ù-mu-un ud-da bar-ru-a mu-zu an-zak-ku*
O father Adad, lord, when the light is darkened, thou declarest thy name.

a-a (see Hymn to Bêl, line 3).
ud-da: *ud* equals *urru*, "light" (Br. 7798, also Hymn to Sin, line 17). *da* is a phonetic complement (see Hymn to Bêl, line 16).
mu-zu an-zak-ku (see on line 1).

8. *a-a* *dimmer* *Mer û-gal-la bar-ru-a mu-zu an-zak-ku*
O father Adad, when the great day is darkened, thou declarest thy name

û-gal-la· *û* (see Hymn to Sin, line 17). *gal-la* (see Hymn to Bêl, line 14).
bar-ru-a: *bar* equals *parâsu*, "cut off" (Br. 1785). The idea "cut", however, is more usually expressed by the value *maš* (see on line 6). *ru*, being a phonetic complement, limits us to the choice of the value *bar* here.

9. *a-a* *dimmer* *Mer uku-gal-la bar-ru-a mu-zu an-zak-ku*
O father Adad, when the great king is cut off, thou declarest thy name.

uku-gal-la: *uku* a value of UG, which is here a Babylonian sign found, for instance, in the Cyrus Cylinder, equals both *ûmu*, "day", and *šarru*, "king" (Br. 3861 and 3862). *gal-la* (see on line 8).

10. *dimmer* *Mer uku An-na bi-maḫ ḫad-ê-a mu-zu an-zak-ku*
O Adad, king of Anu, in the mighty thunder and the lightning flash thou declarest thy name

dimmer *Mer* (see on line 2). *uku* (see MSL 344 and on line 9).

11. *mu-zu kalam-ma mu-un-rù-rù-rù*
Thy name is mightily magnificent in the earth.

mu-zu (see on line 1).
kalam-ma: *kalam* as a value is related to the sign-name KALAMMU and equals *mâtu*, "land" (Br. 5914) We have already had the value *un* (see Hymn to Bêl, line 1). *ma* is a phonetic complement (see Hymn to Bêl, line 1).
mu-un-rù-rù-rù: *mu-un* (see Hymn to Sin, line 17). *rù-rù-rù* (see Hymn to Sin, line 14). A double form like *rù-rù* is common, but the triple form is rare, and expresses a very unusual emphasis.

12. *me-lam-zu kalam-ma tug-gim im-mi-in-dul*
The brightness covers the land like a garment.

me-lam-zu (see Hymn to Bêl, line 21).
kalam-ma (see on line 11).

tug-gim: *tug* equals *ṣubâtu*, "clothing" (Br. 10551). *gim* is an EK form. We have had the ES form *dim* (Hymn to Sin, line 11).

im-mi-in-dul: *im* is an indeterminate verbal prefix, but commonly used for the third person (see Br. p. 545). *mi-in* is a verbal infix, used chiefly of the third person (MSL. pp. XXIV and XXXII). Its antecedent here is *kalam-ma*. *dul* equals *katâmu*, "cover", but *du* also equals *šubtu*, "dwelling" (see Hymn to Bêl, line 14), connoting in both instances the idea "cover, shelter".

13. *za ḫad aka-zu-šù kur-gal a-a* *dimmer* *Mu-ul-lil sag im-da-sig-gi*

The stone of the sceptre of thy thunder strikes the head of the great mountain, father Bêl.

za equals *abnu*, "stone" (Br. 11721 and Hymn to Sin, line 18). There is another sign used more commonly than ZÂU to represent "stone"; namely, DAḲḲU.

ḫad (see on line 1).

aka-zu-šù· *aka* equals *ramâmu*, "roar" (Br. 4746). The meaning of RAM as *ramâmu* seems to come through mnemonic paronomasia by way of the value *aka* as equal to râmu, "love". It is important to distinguish *ramâmu* from *Ramman*, an Assyrian name for *Mer* meaning "thunderer", as well as from *ramânu*, "self". *ramânu* self is often a pun on *Ramman*. *zu* (see Hymn to Bêl, line 21). *šù* (see Hymn to Bêl, line 15)

kur-gal. *kur* (see Hymn to Bêl, line 8). *gal* (see Hymn to Bêl, line 14).

a-a *dimmer* *Mu-ul-lil* (see Hymn to Bêl, line 3). In the Hymn to Bêl (line 16), Bêl seems to be called a mountain. The thought probably is suggested by E-kur of Nippur.

14. *urša-zu àma gal* *dimmer* *Nin-lil ba-e-di-ḫu-laḫ-e*

Thy thunder terrifies the great mother Bêlit.

urša equals *ramâmu* (Br. 8556). *ur* is a value of ḪAR which itself may mean *ramâmu* (Br. 8539) and *ša* is a value of DU which we know means *alâku*. *urša* must mean "advancing thunder".

àma equals *ummu*, "mother". The idea of "mother" arises out of "amplitude", which the sign is intended pictorially to represent. *damal* is a common value of the same sign (see Hymn to Bêl, line 10).

gal (Hymn to Bêl, line 14).

dimmer *Nin-lil*. *Nin-lil* is the Sumerian name of Bêlit, the consort of Bêl. *Nin* equals *Bêltu*, "lady". *lil* has the same meaning as in *En-lil* or *Mul-lil* (see Hymn to Bêl, line 2). *Nin-lil* is exactly the reverse with respect to sex of *En-lil*. Bêlit, like Bêl, had a temple at Nippur which dates back apparently to the time of the early dynasties of Ur. It was, however, simply a dim shadow of the temple of Bêl. The goddess of the divine family never achieved the popularity attained by the god, the father of the family. Besides being called *Nin-lil*, "lady of mercy" (Br. 5932), she was sometimes called *Nin-ḫar-sag*, "lady of the high mountain", which would indicate that she dwelt with Bêl in *E-kur*, "the mountain house". Under the name of *Nin-ḫar-sag*, Bêlit had a temple also at Girsu, one of the divisions of the town of Lagaš. *Nin-ḫar-sag* was sometimes addressed as "the mother of the gods".

ba-e-di-ḫu-láḫ-e is a verb. *ba* is an indeterminate verbal prefix. Here it is third person (see Hymn to Bêl, line 25). *e* (see Hymn to Bêl, line 18). *di* is an unusual infix; it is probably used here in the interest of vowel harmony for *da* (see Hymn to Bêl, line 16). *ḫu-láḫ* is the verb itself and is equal to *galâtu*, "frighten" (Br. 2076). On closer analysis, *ḫu* must be a prefix of generalization; for example *ḫu* may equal *amêlu*, "man" (Br. 2050). *láḫ* must be the real verb; it is equal to *galâtu* (Br. 6166). *e* must be a vowel of prolongation. The usual phonetic complement after *láḫ* is *ḫa*.

The fear of the lightning of Adad in this hymn is somewhat like that expressed in the Babylonian Epic of Gilgameš, Eleventh Tablet. The lord of the storm caused the heavens to rain heavily. There arose from the foundation of heaven a black cloud. The thunderbearers marched over mountain and plain, and Ninib continued pouring out rain and Adad's violence reached to heaven. The southern blast blew hard. Like a battle-charge upon mankind the waters rushed. One could no longer see an other. The gods were dismayed at the flood. They sought refuge by ascending the highest heaven, cowering like dogs. On the battlements of heaven thy crouched and Ištar screamed like a woman in travail.

15. *dingir En-lil-li dumu-ni dimmer Mer-ra à mu-un-da-an-aka*
Bêl to his son Mer measures out power:

dingir En-lil-li: Bêl's name has appeared before in this hymn, but in the ES form (line 13). *dingir En-lil* (see Hymn to Sin, line 5). *li* (see Hymn to Bêl, line 23).

dumu-ni: (see on line 3). *ni* (see Hymn to Bêl, line 13).

à (see Hymn to Bêl, line 14) = ID.

mu-un-da-an-aka. *mu-un* (see Hymn to Sin, line 17). *da-an* is a verbal infix (MSL. pp. XXIV and XXXII). Its antecedent here is *dumu-ni*. *aka*: we have had *aka* equal to *ramâmu* (line 13), but here we have *aka* equal to *madâdu*, "measure out". *madâdu*, "measure out", is a pun on *madâdu*, "love" (thus MSL. p. 21).

16. *mulu dumu-mu û um-me-ši-si-si û um-me-ši-lá-lá*

Thou who art my son, the day thou didst lift up the eye, the day thou didst look!

mulu: The sign is the usual ideogram for "man", but may stand for the Assyrian *ša*, as here. Note that the sign takes the value *lu* in composition (see Hymn to Bêl, line 20).

dumu-mu: *dumu* (see line 3). *mu* is a suffix of the first person (Br. 1241). There are three pronominal *mu's*. First, the determinate pronominal suffix *mu* of the first person, cognate with *ma-e*, the personal pronoun of the first person; this is the *mu* we have here. Secondly, there is a *mu* of *mu-un*, the indeterminate verbal prefix. *mun* or *mu-un* is simply this *mu* nasalized. We have had this *mu* quite often. Finally, there is another *mu*, an indeterminate suffix, which is related to *mu* of *mu-un*, rather than to *mu*, the cognate of *ma-e*. This indeterminate *mu* is found at the end of relative clauses. We shall meet it in the Hymn to Tammuz (see below).

û (see Hymn to Sin, line 17).

um-me-ši-si-si is a verb. *um-me* is a indeterminate verbal prefix, but is chosen here for the second person, since *mu-un* is so often used for the third person. *umme* is not a very common prefix. It stands for *ume* which is a shortened form of *umeni*. *ši*: ŠI with the value *ige* or *ide* we have seen equals *înu*, "eye" (see Hymn to Sin, line 16). *ši* here, however, seems to be regarded as a part of the verbal stem and hence slips in between the prefix and the root. *si-si* (see Hymn to Bêl, line 22). The Sumerian idiom means "fill the eye".

um-me-ši-lá-lá: *um-me-ši* (just explained). *lá-lá*: *lá* is a value of LALLU which occurs as a phonetic complement in the word *En-lil-lá* (Hymn to Sin, line 5) also equals *našû*, "lift up" (Br. 10101).

17. *dimmer Mer-ri û um-me-ši-si-si û um-me-ši-lá-lá*

O Adad, the day thou didst lift up the eye, the day thou didst look!

dimmer Mer (see on line 2). *ri* (see Hymn to Bêl, line 19). *û um-me-ši-si-si û um-me-ši-lá-lá* (see on line 16).

18. *û iminna-bi-meš ba-gan-tal-lá û um-me-ši-lá-lá*

During those seven days thou didst blow a full blast, when thou didst look.

û (see Hymn to Sin, line 17).

iminna-bi-meš: *iminna* is the Sumerian word for "seven". The sign in our text consists of seven uprights, four above and three below. The Assyrian form consists of three above, three in the middle and one at the bottom. *bi* is the demonstrative pronoun

= "those" (Br. 5134 and Hymn to Sin, line 27). *meš* is the Sumerian sign of the plural number (Br. 10470) The sign is composed of ME and EŠ and means "many".

ba-gan-tal-lá: *ba* (see on line 14); *ba* = prefix. *gan* is an infix here of adverbial and corroborative character (see Hymn to Bêl, line 9). *tal* is a value of RI equal to *zâḳu*, "blow" (Br. 2581). We assume *tal* to be the correct value because of the following LALLU = *lá* (see on line 16).

û um-me-ši-lá-lá (see line 16). This interesting statement on the flood agrees entirely with the story of the flood in the Eleventh Tablet of the Babylonian Epic of Gilgameš. The difference between the length of the Hebrew and that of the Babylonian deluge is significant. The narrative of Pirnapištim, the Babylonian Noah, is quite graphic. He represents the gods as seated weeping, their lips covered in fear. Six days and nights the wind blew. When the seventh day appeared, the storm subsided, the sea began to dry and the flood was ended He looked upon the sea, mankind was turned to clay, corpses floated like reeds. He opened the window. He sent forth a dove which returned. He sent forth a raven, which saw the carrion on the water, ate, and wandered away, but did not return. He built an altar on the peak of the mountain and set forth vessels by sevens. The gods smelled the savour and gathered to the sacrifice, and the great goddess lifted up the rainbow which Anu had created. Those days he thought upon and forgot not.

19. *û ì di-zu-ka ḫàr-ḫa-ra ab-ba û um-me-ši-lá-lá*
It was the day of the word of thy judgment, O bull-god of the abyss, the day thou didst look.

û (line 16).

ì equals *amâtu*, "word" (Br. 518, see also Hymn to Sin, line 16).

di-zu-ka: *di* equals *dênu*, "judgment" (Br. 9525 and Hymn to Bêl, line 7) *zu* (Hymn to Bêl, line 21). *ka* = *nota genitivi* (Hymn to Bêl, line 1).

ḫàr-ḫa-ra is the same as *ḫàr-ḫar-a* *ḫàr* is a value of GUṬṬU, meaning *ḳardu*, "heroic one" (MSL. p. 174). We have had the sign with the value *gù* (Hymn to Bêl, line 9). *ḫa-ra*, phonetic representation of *ḫàr-a*, with the same meaning as *ḫàr* of GUṬṬU, plus phonetic complement.

ab-ba: *ab* equals *tâmtu*, "sea" (Br. 3822). The common word for "sea" is AB.ZU, written ZU.AB, meaning "sea of wisdom", the abode of Ea, the god of wisdom. *ab* also equals *aptu*, "abyss" (Br. 3815). *ab*, "sea", or "abyss" is a shortened form of *a-ab*, "water enclosure", "water space". AB with the value *éš* we have had (Hymn to Sin, line 10).

û um-me-ši-lá-lá (line 16).

20. *nim-gir luḫ su-ši-šù mu-ra-du-ud*

As the lightning, a messenger for terror, thou didst go.

nim-gir equals *birḳu*, "lightning" (Br. 9020). *nim-gir* literally means "high lightning". *nim* equals *elû*, "high". *gir* alone equals *birḳu* (Br. 306). The sign GIRÛ in its primitive form is a picture of a "dagger". From the conception of the "dagger", there is, of course, but a short step to that of the forked lightning.

luḫ equals *sukkallu*, "messenger" (Br. 6170). We have had the sign SUKKALLU with the value *laḫ* (line 14, *laḫ*, and Hymn to Sin, line 27).

su-ši-šù equals noun *su-ši* and postposition *šù*. *su-ši*: SU.ŠI means "increase of eye" and equals *šalummatu* which means "splendour", or perhaps "terror". SU.ŠI might be read *su-lim*. SU.ZI, however, has the same meaning (see Br. 235 and 187, also MSL. p. 298), proving the reading SU.ŠI.

mu-ra-du-ud: *mu* (see Hymn to Bêl, line 18). *ra* is an infix of adverbial character denoting motion (MSL. p. XXIV). *du-ud* is no doubt for *du-du*, an intensified form of *du* (see Hymn to Bêl, line 23, *gin*).

21. *mulu dumu-mu rù gin-na-gin-na a-ba zi-gi-en te-ga*

When thou who art my son goest violently about, who can attack like thee!

mulu dumu-mu (see on line 16).

rù equals *naḳâpu*, "break forth violently", or "storm furiously", (Br. 9144). Here we come near to the primary idea of the sign which is that of "the goring bull" (see Hymn to Sin, line 14).

gin-na-gin-na: DU = *alâku* may have any one of three values, *gin*, *tum* or *rà* (Br. 4871). *gin* is the correct value here, as is shown by the phonetic complement *na*. The value *du* must be closely related to *tum* and *gin*. *du* by change of *d* to *t* and by addition of the nasal *m* becomes *tum*. *tum* by change of *t* to *g*, of *u* to *i* and of *m* to *n* becomes *gin*.

a-ba equals *mannu*, "who" (Br. 11370). See also below.

zi-gi-en probably is a phonetic and dialectic form for *za-e-gim* (line 22).

te-ga: *te* equals *ṭeḫû*, "attack" (Br. 7688). *ga*: BA is probably dialectic for *ga* (Br. 103) which would be the same as PISANNU, i. e., *bašû*, "being", or *šakânu*, "establishing".

Reverse

22. *ki-bala ḫul gíg a-a muḫ-zu-šù a-ba za-e-gim te-ga*
The troublesome evil hostile land, O father, which is against thee, who like thee can attack!

ki-bala: *ki* (see Hymn to Bêl, line 9). *bala* equals *palû*, "weapon" (Br. 276). From the idea of "weapon", it is easy to pass to that of "hostility", expressed by *nukurtu* (Br. 272).

ḫul equals *limnu*, "bad" (see Br. 9502 and Hymn to Sin, line 16, *ḫùl*).

gíg equals *marṣu*, "sick" (Br. 9235). The sign is composite, the principal element of which is MI meaning "black".

a-a (see Hymn to Bêl, line 3).

muḫ-zu-šù: *muḫ* equals *eli*, "upon", or "against" (Br. 8841). *zu* (Hymn to Bêl, line 21). *šù* (Hymn to Bêl, line 15) governs the phrase *muḫ-zu*.

a-ba (see on line 21).

za-e-gim: *za-e* (see Hymn to Bêl, line 16). *gim* (see line 12).

te-ga (see on line 21).

23. *ná imi tur-tur-e šú-um-me-ti a-ba za-e-gim te-ga*
The little stone of the storm do thou take. Who can attack like thee!

ná: DAḲḲU has three values for *abnu*, "stone", *za*, *ṣi* and *ná*. We have also had the sign ZA with the value *za* equal to *abnu* (line 13). No doubt DAḲḲU indicates "hailstone" here.

imi is the common value of the sign IMMU for *šâru*, "storm" (Br. 8369).

tur-tur-e: *tur* (see Hymn to Sin, line 28, *ban-da*). The sign is DUMU (lines 3, 15 and 16). *e* (see Hymn to Bêl, line 3).

šú-um-me-ti: *šú* is a part of the verbal conjugation (see Hymn to Bêl, line 25), making it causal. *um-me* (see on line 16). *ti* equals *laḳû*, "take" (Br. 1700). This is the same word as *ti* meaning "life" (Hymn to Bêl, line 16).

a-ba za-e-gim te-ga (see on line 22).

24. *ná gal-gal-e šú-um-me-ti a-ba za-e-gim te-ga*
The large stone do thou take. Who like thee can attack!

ná (see on line 23).

gal-gal-e: *gal* (see Hymn to Bêl, line 14). *e* (see Hymn to Bêl, line 3).

šú-um-me-ti a-ba za-e-gim te-ga (see line 23).

25. *ná tur-tur-zu ná gal-gal-zu muḫ-ba ù-me-ám*
Thy little stone, thy large stone, on it (the land) let it be!

ná (see on line 23).

gal-gal-zu: *gal* (see Hymn to Bêl, line 14). *zu* (Hymn to Bêl, line 21).

tur-tur-zu: *tur* (see on line 23).

muḫ-ba: *muḫ* (see line 22). *ba* is a pronominal suffix of the third person singular (Br. 114).

ù-me-ám verb in the imperative mood. *ù-me*, the same as *um-me* (line 16). *ám* (see Hymn to Bêl, line 12).

26. *ki-bala-a zi-da-zu ù-mu-e-gul da bur su ù-mu-e-se*
The hostile land thy right hand destroys. It gives complete destruction (?)

ki-bala-a (see on line 22). *a* (see Hymn to Bêl, line 9).

zi-da-zu: *zi* equals *imnu*, "right hand" (Br. 2312). *da* is a phonetic complement (see Hymn to Bêl, line 4). *zu* (see Hymn to Bêl, line 21).

ù-mu-e-gul: *ù* is an indeterminate verbal prefix; it is used of the third person (Br. p. 547; see also Hymn to Bêl, line 1). *mu-e* constitutes a double verbal infix, the *mu* being pronominal and the *e* adverbial. *mu* (see line 16 and Hymn to Bêl, line 18). *e* (see Hymn to Bêl, line 18). *gul* equals *abâtu*, "destroy" (Br. 8954).

da equals *idu*, "strength" (see Hymn to Bêl, line 16). *bur* equals *nasâḫu*, "tear away" (Br. 7528). The sign SÎRU occurs only here in all of the four hymns of this Thesis. *su* is the common word for "body", represented by *zumru* (Br. 172). This translation is only provisional.

ù-mu-e-se: *ù-mu-e* (just explained) *se* equals *nadânu*, "give" (Br. 4418). Brünnow gives to the sign the value *sí*, when it stands for *nadânu*.

27. *dimmer Mer-ri dug-dug-ga a-a muḫ-na-šù geš-ni ba-ši-in-ag*
Adad, when he speaks (to one), O father, on him he imposes his government.

dimmer Mer-ri (see on line 17).

dug-dug-ga is a *ḫal*-clause equal to "in commanding". *dug* (see Hymn to Sin, line 15).

a-a (see Hymn to Bêl, line 3).

muḫ-na-šù: *muḫ* (see line 22). *na*, pronominal suffix of the third person (see Hymn to Bêl, line 1). *šù* (see Hymn to Bêl, line 15).

geš-ni: *geš* equals *šutêšuru*, "government" (Br. 5706). *ni* Hymn to Bêl, line 13).

ba-ši-in-ag: *ba* (see Hymn to Bêl, line 25). Sufix *ši-in* (see Hymn to Sin, line 16). *ag* (see Hymn to Bêl, line 25).

28. *a-a* ^{dimmer} *Mer è-ta ê-a-ni û ì di na-nam*

Father Adad, when he comes out of the house he fixes the day of judgment.

è-ta: *è* (see Hymn to Sin, line 3) *ta* (see Hymn to Bêl, line 15).

ê-a-ni: *ê* (see Hymn to Bêl, line 15). *a* is a vowel of prolongation, which *ê* is accustomed to take (see Hymn to Bêl, line 9). *ni* (see (Hymn to Bêl, line 13).

û (see Hymn to Sin, line 17).

ì (see on line 19).

di (see on line 19).

na-nam: *na* is an indeterminate verbal prefix (see MSL. p. XXIV and Hymn to Bêl, lines 1 and 18) *nam* evidently a verb here, equals *šimtu*, "fixing" (Br. 2103)

29. *è-ta eri-ta ê-a-ni uku ban-da na-nam*

When he comes out of the house out of the city, he fixes the mighty day.

è-ta (see on line 28).

eri-ta: *eri* (see Hymn to Bêl, line 13).

ê-a-ni (see on line 28).

uku (see on line 9).

ban-da equals *ekdu*, "strong" (Br. 4127). *ban-da*, following the idea "strength", also equals "young" (see Hymn to Sin, line 28).

na-nam (see line 28).

30. *eri-ta an-na-ta gar-ra-ni û ì ḫar-ra na-nam*

When he establishes himself out of the city, out of heaven, he fixes the day of curse.

eri-ta (see line 29.

an-na-ta: *an-na* (see Hymn to Bêl, line 18). *ta* (see Hymn to Bêl, line 15).

gar-ra-ni: *gar* equals *šakânu*, "establish" (Br. 11978). *ra*, phonetic complement, (Hym to Bêl, line 3). *ni* (see line 28).

û (see Hymn to Sin, line 17).

ì (see on line 19).

ḫar-ra: *ḫar* equals *uṣurtu*, "curse" (Br. 8545). *ra*, phonetic complement.

na-nam (see on line 28).

31. . . *êr lim-ma* ^{dimmer} *Mer*

. . . . Hymn to Adad.

Chapter IV

Tablet 29628, Plate 19, Hymn to Tammuz

Obverse

1. *šes-e tuš*(KU)*-e-na eri êr*(A.ŠI)*-ra na-nam*
   To the brother whose dwelling is the city of weeping, thus:
2. *a-kala šes-e tab An-na*
   The mightiness of the brother, the companion of Anu!
3. *a-kala à*(ID)*-ba en* *dimmer* *Dumu*(TUR)*-zi*
   The mightiness of his power, the lord Tammuz!
4. *dumu*(TUR) *è*(BIT)*-gal-a-ni nu mu-un-su*(SUD,SUG)*-ga-mu*
   The son whose temple is not far away!
5. *azag* *dimmer* *Nanâ-ge*(KIT) *è*(BIT) *An-na-ka im-me*
   The shining one of Ištar, who is in the house of Anu!
6. *mulu ú-sun-na-ge*(KIT) *nu mu-un-su-ga-mu*
   The one of plant-germination, who is not far away!
7. *azag* *dimmer* *Nanâ-ge*(KIT) *za* NANNA *Unug*(UNU)-*ki*-*ka im-me*
   The shining one of Ištar, who is the NANNA-stone of Erech!
8. *mulu zib*(KA)*-ba-ra-ge*(KIT) *nu mu-un-su*(SUD,SUG)*-ga-mu*
   The one of speech, who is not far away!
9. *bara-ka azag* *dimmer* *Nanâ-ge*(KIT) *te ki-ka im-me*
   In the temple, the shining one of Ištar, who is the foundation of the land!
10. *mulu ka-áš-ka-sa-ge*(KIT) *nu mu-un-su*(SUD,SUG)*-ga-mu*
    The one of much wine, who is not far away!
11. *azag* *dimmer* *Nanâ-ge*(KIT) *šà*(LIB)*-mu ú-sun mu-un-si-mal*(IG)
    The shining one of Ištar, whose heart is full of plant-production!
12. *mulu ḫul-mal*(IG) *nu mu-un-su-ga-mu*
    The one enduring evil, who is not far away!
13. *dimmer mutin*(GEŠTIN) *An-na-ge*(KIT) *kaš*(BI)*-ra-bi mu-un-šub*(RU)
    The wine-god of Anu, to whom they present their offering!
14. *mulu ú-sun-na-ge*(KIT) *a-na-ám*(A.AN) *šú-ba ab-rù*(UL)
    The one of plant-germination, what does his hand ordain!
15. *mulu zib*(KA)*-ba-ra-ge*(KIT)
    The one of speech!
16. *mulu ka-áš-ka-sa-ge*(KIT)
    The one of much wine!

17. *mulu ḫul-mal*(IG) *a-na-ám*(A.AN) *šú-ba ab-gin*(DU)
The one who endures evil, whither does his hand go!

18. *dimmer mutin*(GEŠTIN) *An-na-ge*(KIT) PAḪÂDU *sigišše-ra mu-un-šub*(RU)*-bi*
The wine-god of Anu, to whom they offer the lamb of sacrifice!

19. *nim-me azag* dimmer *Nanâ-ra* ì(KA) *mu-un-na-ab-e-e*
The lofty one, the shining one of Ištar, to whom they speak!

20. *nim-me ki mu-lu ni ma-ra an-pad-de*(NE) *a-na mu-un-ba-e-e*
The lofty one of earth who is the abundance of the land, to whom they speak! what do they say?

21. è(BIT) *kaš*(BI)*-a-ka* è(BIT) *gurun*(KIL)*-na-ka dumu*(TUR) *mu-lu azag zu-ge*(KIT) *ne-ne mu-un-til-li*
In the house of wine, in the house of fruit, the son, the shining one of wisdom, who indeed lives!

22. *nim-me azag dimmer mutin*(GEŠTIN) *An-na-ge*(KIT) ì(KA) *mu-un-na-ab-e-e*
The lofty one, the shining one, the wine-god of Anu, to whom they speak!

23. *nim-me ki šes ma-ra an-pad-de*(NE) *a-na-ám*(A.AN) *mu-un-ma-al*
The lofty one of earth, the brother of the land, to whom they speak! what is it (that they say)?

Reverse

24. è(BIT) *kaš*(BI)*-a-ka* è(BIT) *gurun*(KIL)*-na-ka dumu*(TUR) *mulu azag zu-ge*(KIT) *sigišše-sag tuk-a-na*
In the house of wine, in the house of fruit, the son, the shining one of wisdom, who has a great sacrifice!

25. *ur-sag* giš *ku-a sag-mal-mal-ge*(KIT)
The hero of great weapons!

26. *dimmer mutin* (GEŠTIN) *An-na-ge*(KIT) *ú-sun-na sag-mal-mal-ge*(KIT)
The wine-god of Anu, the great plant-germinator!

27. *ú-sun gurun*(KIL)*-gurun*(KIL) *ú-sun gurun*(KIL)*-gurun*(KIL) *šes-mu ú-sun gurun*(KIL)*-gurun*(KIL)
The germinator of many fruits, the germinator of many fruits, my brother, the germinator of many fruits!

28. *ú-sun a-ra-li ú-sun gurun*(KIL)*-gurun*(KIL) *šes-mu ú-sun gu-run*(KIL)*-gurun*(KIL)
The germinator of the lower world, the germinator of many fruits, my brother, the germinator of may fruits!

29. *in-nu giš*(UŠ) *giš gu-ga-ge*(KIT) *tàl*(ÀŠ)*-ta-al-ta-al mu-ib-rá* (DU)*-rá*(DU)
The vegetable-germinator, the only plant-begetter, who goeth forth!

30. *dumu*(TUR) *zi-ga-na ga-ni šà*(LIB)*-zi-zi mu-ib-rá*(DU)
The son of life; in his fulness, in the midst of life goeth.

31. *eš diš êr*(A.ŠI)*-lim*(LIB)*-ma dimmer Dumu-zi-da-kam*
Thirty lines. Hymn to Tammuz.

The salient phases of the rounded out Tammuz story are touched upon in this hymn; viz., his local dwelling in a city where he had a temple; the memorial weeping; his relation to Anu; his lordly power; his specification as "a brother"; his relation to the goddess Ištar; his characteristic and supreme function of plant-germination. Note also that he was the agricultural god of spring vegetation. Offerings of wine were poured out over his bier, he having been humbled to sorrow by banishment to the lower world, where he became a lord over the occult and internal forces inherent beneath the soil of the earth. So he became a god of a new life. The hymn does not seem altogether to confine the germinating work of Tammuz to the vegetation of spring growth, but appears, especially in the Reverse, to include fruit growing which might come later in the season. Possibly this hymn was sung as a dirge at Babylonian anniversaries for the departed Tammuz. The Babylonians at the time of the summer solstice annually commemorated with lamentation the departure of Tammuz to the lower world. He had instructed them that they should gather at his bier and that hired musicians should sing and play and that the people should sacrifice and drink wine.

Obverse

1. *šes-e tuš-e-na eri êr-ra na-nam*
To the brother whose dwelling is the city of weeping, thus:

šes-e: *šes* same as *šis* (Hymn to Sin, line 2). *e* equals *ana*, "*to*" (Br. 5847).

tuš-e-na: *tuš* equals *ašâbu*, "dwell" (Br. 10523). Probably the sign has the same value for *šubtu*, "dwelling" (Br. 10553). We have had the sign (KU) with the value *šù* (Hymn to Bêl, line 15). *e*, vowel of prolongation. *na*, pronominal suffix (see Hymn to Adad, line 27).

eri (Hymn to Bêl, line 13).

êr-ra: *êr* (Hymn to Bel, Colophon). *ra*, phonetic complement (Hymn to Bêl, line 3).

na-nam equals *kîam*, "thus" (see Br. 1597 and Hymn to Adad, line 28). The words "O my brother" are represented in legend as being first uttered by the sister of Tammuz and then taken up by other mourners. Probably the custom of weeping for Tammuz originated in the city of Eridu.

2. *a-kala šes-e tab An-na*

The mightiness of the brother, the companion of Anu!

a-kala is an abstract noun like *nam-kala* which is equal to *dannûtu* (Br. 6194). *a* is an abstract prefix, as in A.DU, equal to *a-rá*, "going" (MSL. p. XVII). *kala* equal *dannu*, "mighty" (Br. 6194).

šeš-e. See on *šes* (line 1). *e*, probably sign of the genitive, if not merely a vowel of prolongation. It can certainly be a postposition (see on line 1).

tab (see Hymn to Adad, line 6).

An-na (see Hymn to Adad, line 3 and Hymn to Bêl, line 18). Tammuz was a companion of Giššzida in the dominion of Anu. Giššzida was also a god of vegetable growth. At a certain period of the year, Tammuz and Giššzida were stationed in companionship as attendants at the gate of heaven. Here the power of Tammuz to cause vegetation to grow began to be effective. He was, in the first days of his existence, a sun-god, and, stationed in heaven, the rays of his power were felt on earth. So, probably every year, at the time of spring growth, he was conceived of as operating from heaven like a sun.

3. *a-kala à-ba en* *dimmer* *Dumu-zi*

The mightiness of his power, the lord Tammuz!

a-kala (see on line 2).

à-ba: *à* (see Hymn to Bêl, line 14). *ba* (Hymn to Adad, line 25).

en (see Hymn to Bêl, line 19).

dimmer *Dumu-zi.* *Dumu-zi* means "son of life". *Dumu* (Hymn to Sin, line 5). *zi* (see Hymn to Bêl, line 23).

4. *dumu è-gal-a-ni nu mu-un-su-ga-mu*

The son whose temple is not far away!

dumu (see Hymn to Sin, line 5, *ṭu-mu*).

è-gal-a-ni: *è-gal* equals *êkallu*, "temple", (Br 6252). È.GAL, "great house", is the common compound ideogram for "temple", both in Sumerian and Assyrian. The Assyrian *êkallu* is evidently the Sumerian *è*, plus *gal* which is changed to *kal.* The word has passed over into Hebrew, Syriac and Arabic. *è* (see Hymn to Sin, line 3). *gal* (see Hymn to Bêl, line 14). *è-gal* is often followed by *la*; here, however, it is followed by *a*, showing that the phonetic use of *la* and *a* is quite similar. *ni* (see Hymn to Bêl, line 13).

nu (Hymn to Sin, line 27).

mu-un-su-ga-mu is a verb and seems to mean "who is far away". The clause occurs also in lines six, eight, ten and twelve, only that in lines six and twelve SU is used instead of SUD. *mu-un* (see Hymn to Sin, line 17). *su*: SUD seems to equal *rûḳu*, "distant", here. Yet when it is equal to *rûḳu*, it generally has the value *sud* and is followed by the phonetic complement *da*; here it is followed by *ga*. So the value should be *sug* or *su*. *mu* is a relative suffix related to *mu* of *mu-un* (see Hymn to Adad, line 16).

5. *azag* *dimmer* *Nanâ-ge è An-na-ka im-me*

The shining one of Ištar, who is in the house of Anu!

azag (see Hymn to Sin, line 1).

dimmer *Nanâ-ge*. *Nanâ*, also written *Nanna*, is the Sumerian name of Ištar. NANNU is sometimes written like RI which, when preceded by the god-sign, also equals "Ištar". *ge* (see Hymn to Adad, line 4).

è (see Hymn to Sin, line 3).

An-na-ka (see Hymn to Adad, line 4). *ka* equals *nota genitivi* (see Br. 551 and Hymn to Bêl, line 1).

im-me: *im* (see Hymn to Sin, line 23) *me* (Hymn to Bêl, line 16). Tammuz seems to be the shining one. The epithet "shining" is sometimes applied to gods, goddesses, kings, princes and others. The primary relaltion of Tammuz was that of lover. But in the lower world he made love to another. But each year during the season of vegetable growth he was supposed to be living with Ištar and during the season of vegetable decline he was supposed to be living with the other whom he loved in the regions below. The house of Anu might mean the temple of Anu, but the reference in this line is no doubt to heaven, over which Anu was lord and at whose portals Tammuz sometimes acted as porter.

6. *mulu ú-sun-na-ge nu mu-un-su-ga-mu*

The one of plant-germination, who is not far away!

mulu (see Hymn to Adad, line 16).

ú-sun-na-ge: *ú-sun* seems to be a compound noun meaning "plant-growing". It occurs eight times in the hymn. *ú* equals *šammu*, "plant" (Br. 6027). It is sometime a determinative before the name of a plant (Br. 6029). *sun* means "irrigate" (MSL. 299). It is improbable that this sign is KIB. *ge* (see Hymn to Adad, line 4).

nu (see Hymn to Sin, line 27).

mu-un-su-ga-mu (see line 4). *su*(SU) and *su*(SUD,SUG) are interchangeable (Br. 7593).

7. *azag* ^{dimmer} *Nanâ-ge za* NANNA *Unug-ka im-me*
The shining one of Ištar, who is the NANNA-stone of Erech!

azag ^{dimmer} *Nana-ge* (see on line 5).
za: the probable meaning of *za* here is "stone" (see Hymy to Adad, line 13).

NANNA: there are no citations in Brünnow showing the meaning of NANNA when standing alone. *za*-NANNA-*di* equals *mammû*, "snow", and *ža*-NANNA may mean "white stone". If NANNA can equal UŠLANU-GUNÛ, then it can mean *nasâḳu* (Br. 3019) and *za*-NANNA means "shining stone". It may be that NANNA stands for USLANU-GUNÛ, then ZA.NANNA.UNU.KI could be equal to *Unug*-^{ki} (Br. 11749), and the line would read *azag* ^{dimmer} *Nanâ-ge Unug*-^{ki}-*ka im-me*, "the shining one of Ištar of Erech he is".

Unug: that *Unug* is the correct value is shown by the phonetic complement *ga* that often follows UNU. Erech, we know, was the city of Ištar (Br. 3023). *unu* (see Hymn to Sin, line 2). *ka* (line 5)
im-me (see on line 5).

8. *mulu zib-ba-ra-ge nu mu-un-su-ga-mu*
The one of speech, who is not far away!

mulu (see Hymn to Adad, line 16)
zib-ba-ra-ge: *zib-ba* (see Hymn to Sin, line 16, *gu*). *ra* must answer for vowel prolongation (Hymn to Bêl, line 3). *ge* (see Hymn to Adad, line 4). "One of speech" must mean the god endowed with authoritative utterance on the subject of germination.
nu mu-un-su-ga-mu (see on line 4).

9. *bara-ka azag* ^{dimmer} *Nanâ-ge te ki-ka im-me*
In the temple the shining one of Ištar, who is the foundation of the land!

bara-ka: *bara* equals *parakku*, "dwelling room in the temple" (Br. 6878). *ka* (line 5).
azag ^{dimmer} *Nanâ-ge* (line 5).
te equals *temennu*, "foundation" (Br. 7710).
ki-ka: *ki* (Hymn to Bêl, line 9). *ka* (Hymn to Bêl, line 1).
im-me (line 5)

10. *mulu ka-dáš-ka-sa-ge nu mu-un-su-ga-mu*
The one of much wine, who is not far away!

mulu (see Hymn to Adad, line 16).
ka-dáš is evidently a phonetic representation of *kaš*(BI), cognate with *geš* in *geštin* and equal to *karânu*, "wine" (Br. 5121, 5004 and 5006).

ka-sa-ge: *ka-sa* may be a phonetic form for *kas* equal to *šinâ*, "two" (Br. 4459). Perhaps it would be better to consider *ka-áš ka-sa* as a reduplication of *kaš*, as *kaš-kas(š)* = "much wine". *ge* (Hymn to Adad, line 4). One form of the legend makes Tammuz the begetter of autumn vegetation. If so, he is the producer of much wine. More likely the meaning is that, on his account, much wine was offered in the service of lamentation at his departure.

nu mu-un-su-ga-mu (see on line 4).

11. *azag* ^dimmer^ *Nanâ-ge šà-mu ú-sun mu-un-si-mal*
The shining one of Ištar, whose heart is full of plant-production!

azag ^dimmer^ *Nanâ-ge* (line 5).

šà-mu: *šà* Hymn to Sin, line 9, *šag*). Relative *mu* (see line 4).

ú-sun (line 6).

mu-un-si-mal. *mu-un* (see Hymn to Sin, line 17). *si* (see Hymn to Bêl, line 22). *mal* (see Hymn to Bêl, line 18). Plant growth is a matter of intelligent devising on the part of Tammuz.

12. *mulu ḫul-mal nu mu-un-su-ga-mu*
The one enduring evil, who is not far away!

mulu (see Hymn to Adad, line 16).

ḫul-mal equals *limnu*, "evil" (Br. 9508). *ḫul* equals *limênu*. "be evil". *mal* (Hymn to Bêl, line 18).

nu mu-un-su-ga-mu (line 6).

13. *dimmer mutin An-na-ge kaš-ra-bi mu-un-šub*
The wine-god of Anu, to whom they present their offering!

mutin is "wood of life", *mu* being ES for *geš*, "wood", and *tin* being for *ti* (Hymn to Bêl, line 16).

An-na-ge: *An-na* (see Hymn to Adad, line 3). *ge* (Hymn to Adad, line 4).

kaš-ra-bi: *kaš* equals *šikaru*, "strong drink" (Br. 5126). *ra* answers as a vowel of prolongation (Hymn to Bêl, line 3). If *ra* were a postposition, it would follow the suffix *bi* (on which see Hymn to Sin, line 27).

mu-un-šub: *mu-un* (Hymn to Sin, line 17). *šub* equals *nadû* "cast down" (Br. 1434). RU signifies "bent down". The attitude of the mourners may be noted.

14. *mulu ú-sun-na-ge a-na-ám šú-ba ab-rù*
The one of plant-germination, what does his hand ordain!

mulu ú-sun-na-ge (see line 6).

a-na-ám equals *minammi* (Br. 11436) which is the same as *minû* "what?" (Br. 11434). Note that *a-ba* (Hymn to Adad, line 21) equals *mannu*, "who?"

šú-ba: *šú* (Hymn to Bêl, line 25). *ba* (see Hymn to Adad, line 25).

ab-rù: *ab* (Hymn to Bêl, line 16). *rù* (Hymn to Sin, line 14).

15. *mulu zib-ba-ra-ge*
The one of speech!

See line 8.

16. *mulu ka-áš-ka-sa-ge*
The one of much wine!

See line 10.

17. *mulu ḫul-mal a-na-ám šú-ba ab-gin*
The one who endures evil, whither does his hand go!

mulu ḫul-mal (line 12)
a-na-àm šú-ba (line 14).
ab-gin: *ab* (Hymn to Bêl, line 16). *gin* (Hymn to Bêl, line 23).

18. *dimmer mutin An-na-ge* PAḪÂDU *sigišše-ra mu-un-šub-bi*
The wine-god of Anu, to whom they offer the lamb of sacrifice!

dimmer mutin An-ua-ge (line 13).

PAḪÂDU, Assyrian for "lamb". The sign is PISANNU enclosing GÊSṬARÛ (Br. 5489). The Sumerian value of the sign is not known. Among the few citations in which the sign appears, a female lamb is mentioned (Br. 10946).

sigišše-ra: *sigišše* equals *nîḳû*, "sacrifice", and *ra* answers as a vowel of prolongation which the sign takes (Br. 9092).

mu-un-šub-bi· *mu-un-šub* (line 13). *bi* is a phonetic complement.

19. *nim-me azag* *dimmer* *Nanâ-ra ì mu-un-na-ab-e-e*
The lofty one, the shining one of Ištar, to whom they speak.

nim-me: *nim* (see Hymn to Adad, line 20). *me*, phonetic complement.

azag (Hymn to Sin, line 1.)

dimmer *Nanâ-ra*: *dimmer* *Nanâ* (line 5). *ra* (Hymn to Bêl, line 3).

ì (Hymn to Adad, line 19).

mu-un-na-ab-e-e: *mu-un* (Hymn to Sin, line 17) *na-ab* is a verbal infix = "to him", third person here (MSL. p. XXXII). *e-e* (Hymn to Bêl, line 14).

20. *nim-me ki mu-lu ni ma-ra an-pad-de a-na mu-un-ba-e-e*
The lofty one of the earth who is the abundance of the land, to whom they speak. What doth he say!

nim-me (line 19).
ki (Hymn to Bêl, line 9).
mu-lu (Hymn to Bêl, line 20).
ni (Hymn to Bêl, line 13).

an-pad-de: *an* (Hymn to Adad, line 1). *pad* (Hymn to Sin, line 10). *de*, phonetic complement.

a-na equals *minû*, "what" (Br. 11484), the same as *a-na-ám* (line 14).

mu-un-ba-e-e: *mu-un* (Hymn to Sin, line 17). *ba* may be used as an infix as well as a prefix (MSL. p. XXIV, and Hymn to Bêl, lines 24 and 25). *e-e* (line 19).

21 *è kaš-a-ka è gurun-na-ka dumu mu-lu azag zu-ge ne-ne mu-un-til-li*

In the house of wine, in the house of fruit, the son, the shining one of wisdom, who indeed liveth!

kaš-a-ka: *kaš* (line 13). *a* (Hymn to Bêl, line 9). *ka* (line 5).

gurun-na-ka: *gurun* equals *inbu*, "fruit" (Br. 10179). *na*, phonetic complement. *ka* (just explained).

dumu (Hymn to Sin, line 5).

mu-lu (Hymn to Bêl, line 20).

azag (Hymn to Sin, line 1).

zu-ge: *zu* (Hymn to Bêl, line 1). *ge* (Hymn to Adad, line 4).

ne-ne (Hymn to Bêl, line 21).

mu-un-til-li: *mu-un* (Hymn to Sin, line 17). *til* is probably the longer form of *ti* (Hymn to Bêl, line 16).

22. *nim-me azag dimmer mutin An-na-ge ì mu-un-na-ab-e-e*

The lofty one, the shining one, the wine-god of Anu, to whom they speak!

nim-me azag (line 19).

dimmer mutin An-na-ge (line 13).

ì mu-un-na-ab-e-e (line 19).

23. *nim-me ki šes ma-ra an-pad-de a-na-ám mu-un-ma-al*

The lofty one of earth, the brother of the land, to whom they speak! What doth his hand effect!

nim-me ki (line 20).

šes (line 1).

ma-ra (Hymn to Sin, line 16).

an-pad-de (line 20).

a-na-ám (line 14)

mu-un-ma-al: *mu-un* (Hymn to Sin, line 17). *ma-al* is the verb (Hymn to Bêl, line 11).

Reverse

24. *è kaš-a-ka è gurun-na-ka dumu mulu azag zu-ge sigišše sag tuk-a-na*

In the house of wine, in the house of fruit, the son, the shining one of wisdom, who has a great sacrifice!

è kaš-a-ka è gurun-na-nka dumu mulu azag zu-ge (line 21).
sigišše (line 18).
sag (Hymn to Bêl, line 5).
tuk-a-na: *tuk* equals *išû*, "have" (Br. 11237). *a*, vowel of prolongation (Hymn to Bêl, line 9). *na*, suffix of the third person (Hymn to Bêl, line 1).

25. *ur-sag* *giš* *ku-a sag-mal-mal-ge*
The hero of great weapons!

ur equals *amêlu*, "man" (Br. 11256).
sag (Hymn to Bêl, line 5). *ur-sag* means "head-man", and is also equal to *ḳarradu*, "mighty one".
giš *ku-a*: *giš* equals *iṣu*, "wood", and is a determinative before names of things made of wood. *ku* equals *bêlu*, "weapon", perhaps sacrificial implements. *a*, vowel of prolongation.
sag-mal-mal-ge: *sag* (just explained). *mal-mal*: PISANNU is dialectic for either MA.AL or IḲU and as a suffix makes an adjective of a noun (see Hymn to Bêl, lines 1 and 18) *ge* (see Hymn to Adad, line 4).

26. *dimmer mutin An-na-ge ú-sun-na sag-mal-mal-ge*
The wine god of Anu, the great plant-germinator!

dimmer mutin An-na-ge (line 13).
ú-sun-na (line 6).
sag mal-mal-ge (line 25).

27. *ú-sun gurun-gurun ú-sun gurun-gurun šes-mu ú-sun gurun-gurun*
The germinator of many fruits, the germinator of many fruits, my brother, the germinator of many fruits!

ú-sun (line 6).
gurun-gurun, plural form of *gurun* (line 21).
šes-mu: *šes* (line 1). *mu* (Hymn to Adad, line 16).

28. *ú-sun a-ra-li ú-sun gurun-gurun šes-mu ú-šun gurun-gurun*
The germinator of the lower world, the germinator of many fruits, my brother, the germinator of many fruits!

ú-sun (line 6).
a-ra-li has passed over into Assyrian as *arallû*, "lower world". *a-ra-li* is phonetic. There is a sign, URUGAL, translated by *arallû*. URUGAL consists of the "enclosure" sign containing the sign GAL and means "great house". *è-kur-be* is also translated by *arallû* and is equal to *bît mûti*, "house of the dead" (Br. 6259); more literally the meaning is "house of the land of the dead".
ú-sun gurun-gurun šes-mu (line 27).

29. *in-nu gíš* ^{giš}*-gu-ga-ge tàl-ta-al-ta-al mu-ib-rá-rá*
The vegetable germinator(?), the only plant begetter, who goeth forth!

in-nu might equal *tibnu*, "straw", "vegetation" (Br. 4231). Perhaps it would be better to take *in-nu* as a verb meaning "he is the one who", *in* being a verbal prefix and *nu* the verbal stem in the sense of *zikaru* (Br. 1964), as in *nu-banda* (MSL. 264).

gíš: UŠ with the value *gíš* equals *riḫû*, "beget" (Br. 5042).

^{giš}*gu-ga-ge*: ^{giš} (see line 25). *gu* (Hymn to Bêl, line 20). *ga* answers as a vowel of prolongation. *ge* (Hymn to Adad, line 4).

tàl-ta-al-ta-al: *tàl* is the value of ÁŠ required by the phonetic gloss *ta-al-ta-al*.

mu-ib-rá-rá: *mu* (see Hymn to Bêl, line 18). *ib* is a modal verbal infix (MSL. p. XXIV). *rá* is a value of DU (see Hymn to Adad, line 21, *gin*).

30. *dumu zi-ga-na ga-ni šà-zi-zi mu-ib-rá*
The son of life, his fulness in the midst of life goeth forth.

dumu (Hymn to Sin, line 5).

zi-ga-na: *zi* (Hymn to Bêl, line 23). *ga* serves for vowel prolongation. *na* is postpositional.

ga-ni: *ga* (Hymn to Bêl, line 12). *ni* may be taken as the possessive suffix of the third person.

šà-zi-zi: *šà* (Hymn to Bêl, line 22). *zi* (just explained)

mu-ib-rá (see line 29).

31. *eš diš êr-lim-ma* ^{dimmer}*Dumu-zi-da-kam*
Thirty lines. Hymn to Tammuz.

eš: GÊŠPÛ with the value *eš* means "thirty". *diš* is frequently a determinative before proper names, but here seems to mean "line".

êr lim-ma (see Hymn to Bêl, colophon).

^{dimmer}*Dumu-zi-da-kam*· ^{dimmer}*Dumu-zi* (line 3). *da* (Hymn to Bêl, line 4). *kam* (Hymn to Sin, line 27).

Glossary

Lightning Source UK Ltd.
Milton Keynes UK
UKHW022106080223
416681UK00011B/2826

9 781016 282178